1979

D1568447

WIRE
ART

OTHER BOOKS BY THE AUTHORS
Kite Craft
Plastics for the Craftsman

with Thelma R. Newman
The Frame Book
Paper as Art and Craft

WIRE

ART

Metals · Techniques · Sculpture · Collage
Jewelry · Mixed Media

Jay Hartley Newman
Lee Scott Newman

CROWN PUBLISHERS, INC., NEW YORK

PREFACE

Wire holds many surprises for the artist and craftsman. Although it is an ancient material, we rarely think of it as a pure medium—as a material to be worked alone for what it has to offer. To the jewelers, of course, wire's integrity has long been common knowledge. Wire is more versatile than most of us realize.

Versatility is what this book is about. Our point is simple: that wire is an essential material. It is pure. It is easy to work skillfully. It is inexpensive. Most important, it has illimitable potential. Wire has dimension. It defines space as a line does—with all the invention and dimension artists have ever put into their lines.

Alone, wire finds applications in hundreds of processes and products. In combination with other media, products still rely on wire's unique characteristics and capabilities. The range of wire materials and their plasticity make this possible. Wires are available in almost every metal—gold, silver, platinum, copper, brass, aluminum, iron, tin, steel. And in every metal they come in many forms from the finest filamentous strand to heavy rods and tubes.

With this richness, we have only sought to explore the few basic, but necessary, methods of working wires successfully. We touch upon most of the essential techniques. Many will be perceived intuitively and through exploration. Along with the methods we offer a collection of the forms we feel to be significant and credit-worthy wire possibilities. This, we hope, will only begin to suggest the potentialities of an ancient, yet modern, material. We hope, too, that artists and craftsmen will recognize—as so many have before them—that wire springs eternal.

Inquiries should be addressed to Crown Publishers, Inc., 419 Park Avenue South, New York, N.Y. 10016.

Printed in the United States of America
Published simultaneously in Canada by
General Publishing Company Limited
Design by Nedda Balter

Library of Congress Cataloging in Publication Data
Newman, Jay Hartley.
    Wire art.

    Bibliography: p.
    Includes index.
    1. Wire craft. I. Newman, Lee Scott, joint author.
II. Title.
TT214.3.N48   745.56   74–32448
ISBN 0–517–51622–5

ACKNOWLEDGMENTS

A book such as *Wire Art* owes its existence to the imagination and energy of countless people who have contributed to the art and craft of wireworking throughout the ages. Many individuals, institutions, and galleries have helped us, and the information and works gathered here could never have been compiled without their generous cooperation.

Extraordinary thanks go to Mary Lee Hu, Maurice Abramson, Clifford Earl, and Mitchell Egenberg. We are, as ever, extremely grateful to Norm Smith for a beautiful job of photo processing.

Most of all, continuing thanks go to our wonderful parents, Jack and Thelma Newman. Their help and encouragement in everything are unfailing and unending. Our debt to them is the greatest.

The individuals, galleries, and institutions listed below were all helpful in developing this book:

American Craftsman's Council
Art Institute of Chicago
William Bowie
Nancy Cohen
Eva Cossack
Rudy Dorval
Fairweather Hardin Gallery
Herbert A. Feuerlicht
William Harper
Honeywell
Kennedy Galleries
Norbert Kricke
Lefebre Gallery
Robert Leibel
Los Angeles County Museum

Thomas Markusen
Marlborough Gallery
Brigitte & Martin Matschinsky-Denninghoff
Metropolitan Museum of Art
Museum of Modern Art
Museum of Primitive Art
A. Alan Perkins
George Rickey
Mary Ann Scherr
Robert Spooner
Staempfli Gallery
Tate Gallery
Vassar College Art Gallery
Victoria & Albert Museum
Willard Gallery

J. H. N.
L. S. N.

All photographs are by the authors and Thelma R. Newman unless otherwise credited.

*For Jody Lanard
and William Zinsser*

CONTENTS

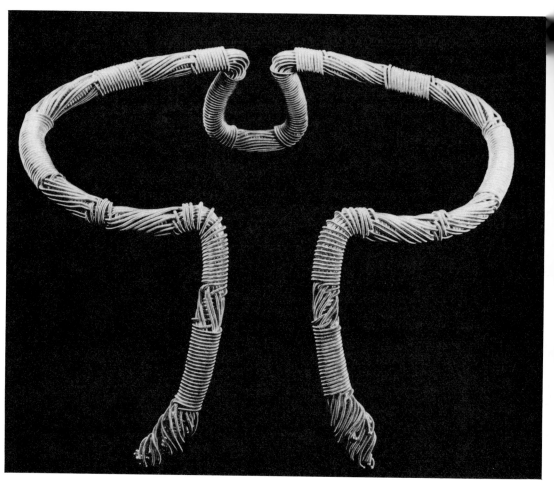

Neckpiece #6 (1969), by Mary Lee Hu, of fine and sterling silver wires. Courtesy: Mary Lee Hu.

Chapter 1

WIRE NOT?

Wire is ubiquitous. Whether as thin as a filament or as enduring as a steel cable, wire figures importantly in the technology and aesthetics of this age. Benjamin Franklin discovered electricity by flying a kite on a wire line. Today, that same electricity is harnessed on millions of miles of wire that carries current from source to use all over the world. Tungsten filaments make incandescent light possible. Much of our engineering depends upon wire mesh and wire rods for reinforcement. The springs supporting nearly every mode of land transportation from horse-drawn buggy to high-speed trains are often wire products. Our motors depend upon wire

The Masai of southern Kenya use wire directly in bracelets and arm coils. They string beads on wire as well.

coils to develop magnetic fields, and wire lines support telephone poles, buildings, and suspension bridges.

Our civilization seems preoccupied with utilizing wire for technical progress. But the earliest applications of wires were clearly not technological, but ornamental. Even today, men in more primitive cultures often rely upon wire as structure and ornament. Contemporary artists, as well, work in wire.

Wire appeals to artisans because it is elemental. A wire rod is an indivisible structural unit. Wire calls to mind the line—a line in space, a line in a plane: infinitely variable. Like the line, wire can extend infinitely. It may be stretched and twisted in a single plane, undulating, swerving, and dipping to define two-dimensional images. But wire is capable of more than two-dimensional interpretations of three-dimensional masses and voids. Wire, unlike the theoretical line, is real. Wire has shape. Escaping from the plane, wire defines space.

For the craftsman and artist, the purity of form offered by wire has not been forgotten. Wire is a basic medium that frees us of restrictions which some other media impose. Wire can be as strong as steel, or as fine and fragile as a hair. Wire can be inexpensive and disposable, but it may be precious when drawn of gold or platinum. Wire may be readily formed with few and simple tools, or wire may be worked with elaborate equipment in sophisticated techniques. Wire products may be permanent, or doodles of the moment.

Although wire is an ancient material, the techniques of working it have remained surprisingly similar to this day. We have refined our tools. We have developed finer and stronger wire; we have found stronger solders and more complicated chemical treatments, but the essential methods are immutable. Wire must be cut, forged, bent, twisted, crumpled, crimped, stretched, drawn, annealed, joined, soldered, cast. The means of working this continuous strand of metal remain quite constant.

The beauty of wire is that almost all those techniques are easily learned. Some we come by easily—like bending or twisting a strand of

Richard Lippold's Flight (1962, 30' x 80' x 40') defines space in New York's Pan Am building. Fine filaments of steel wire are strong enough to span large distances. They create an illusion of volume. The forms vary as light strikes the wires from different angles and in different intensities. Courtesy: Willard Gallery.

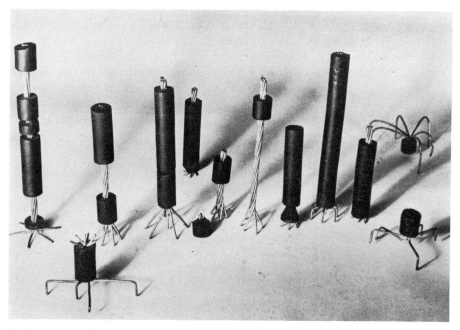

Herbert Feuerlicht constructs Moon People© by stripping insulation from wire cable and spreading the wires. Courtesy: Herbert A. Feuerlicht.

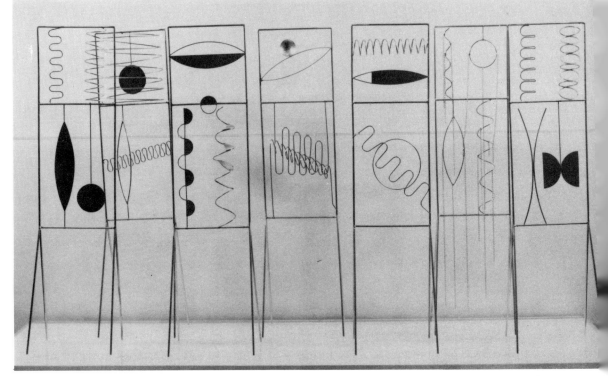

Fausto Melotti builds precious objects in gold wire. Courtesy: Marlborough Gallery.

wire (the fate of many uninspired paper clips). Forging (or hammering), too, is familiar. Soldering requires only a little practice.

The skill of wireworking involves combining these basic techniques and working this essential material with imagination as well as technical competence. Technical mastery comes quickly. The art of wireworking lies less in rote performance of the method than it does in coordination of techniques.

Perceiving combinations of material and technique is a skill that can be learned by experimenting with materials and exploring systematically many facets of their individual characteristics. Wire suits such explorations wonderfully, because it is easily purchased and often more easily found: in coat hangers, discarded electrical equipment, used bailings.

WIRE MANUFACTURE

Wire's origin remains unknown, but its manufacture dates back thousands of years. Nearly as old as metal itself, the first wires were probably made by hammering around a bar so that the metal was stretched out thinner and thinner, eventually resulting in a fine continuous strand of metal.

The current manufacturing process, *wiredrawing*, was developed seven hundred years ago in medieval France, where wire was needed for construction of chain-mail armor used by the knights.

Blocks of metal first go through a rough shaping process, which in

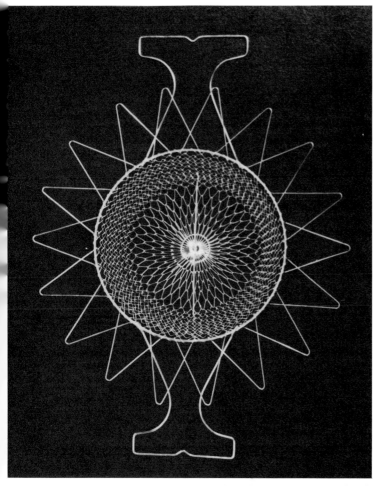

A French salad strainer uses interlaced wires to contain food-stuffs. The structure is flexible, making it easy to store.

medieval times was done by hand hammering the metal. Today, rolling mills compress and stretch the metal while it is hot. The actual process of drawing is carried out when the metal is cool.

One end of the roughly shaped rod is filed down so that it will fit through a hole in the *drawplate,* a steel plate with a series of holes of successively decreasing diameter. Lubricated by beeswax, the metal is drawn through the holes in series with the aid of special tongs. Drawing may continue until the metal reaches the fineness desired, or until the metal is as thin as possible. Different substances have different compression qualities, and not all may be drawn as thin as gold and platinum.

A crucial part of the drawing process is *annealing,* or heating. Every time the metal is drawn through the plate it is compressed and stretched. It becomes brittle, hard. In order to soften the wire and relieve this stress it is heated. The heat softens the metal. Wire need not, however, be heated every time it is drawn through a hole. In fact, craftsmen often draw wire precisely to stiffen it for certain applications.

Drawplates serve other purposes, too. In addition to helping make

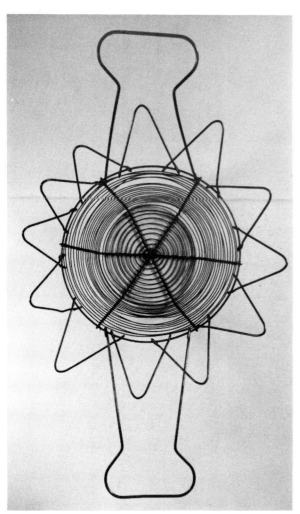

Another version of the kitchen basket is completely rigid. A spiraled cylinder of wire is held to the six-spoke frame by thin binding wires.

wire, plates are used to shape and reshape wire. Holes can be any of a hundred different shapes. The most common shapes are round, half round, oval, half oval, octagonal, hexagonal, rectangular, and square.

THE WIRE POTENTIAL

The pieces selected for this chapter represent a broad range of wires, uses, and design solutions. Included are ornaments made and worn by the Masai of southern Kenya. The Masai use wire in and of itself and, simultaneously, as an armature for networks of fine glass beads. Here, too, is a relic of ancient Greece: a classic form that has survived the ages in corpus and spirit as well. Contemporary jewelry by Mary Lee Hu illustrates her use of timeless techniques to create truly modern forms. Wire, with the insulation still on it, becomes "Moon People" in the eyes of Herbert Feuerlicht. For others, highly polished steel glistens cleanly on a suspension of fine wire legs. To Pol Bury, wire is fine art form and a source of amusement; his fine strands of wire move imperceptibly with the aid of motors—they challenge our perception. Soto also finds wire's linear motion exciting when combined with graphic design. Calder teases us with funny forms outlining animals and faces of friends. Wire objects are found in the kitchen; wire whisks and salad baskets are efficient, functional, and handsome design solutions. Sculptors see wire in many ways. Len Lye allows long strands to sway freely. Dusan Dzamonja combines hundreds of short stumps in dense geometric configurations.

Surprise comes in the realization that although every form is different, the processes involved in creating each remain simple and few in number. Our emphasis here is just that: the ease with which wire may be worked skillfully. Unlike with some materials, the technical obstacles to working with wire are minimal. Our focus must be as much to explore the wire vocabulary for inspiration as to broaden our knowledge.

This survey of wire forms spans ranges of time, space, image, culture, and imagination. The processes repeat themselves, but the forms do not. Wire's potential is immense, and results will never cease to be startling and satisfying, because from wire springs a wealth of possibilities.

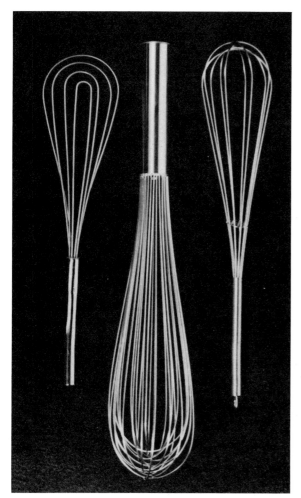

Wire whisks provide another example of fine and functional design in prosaic housewares.

Group Process (1971), by J. H. Newman, utilizes flexible wire springs as vehicles for polyester light bulbs.

Square wire may be transformed into dynamic form by forging. Copyright by Herbert A. Feuerlicht.

Wire lends itself often to the linear and the angular as suggested by a radio tower viewed from underneath.

In Norbert Kricke's own words, he uses wire "as line, always to show space and time. Lines are never used in a way to make contours of mass-form." Courtesy: Norbert Kricke.

In New Jersey Meadows (1964, 12' x 12' x 8'), Richard Lippold uses filamentous strands to evoke the image of grasses and reeds swaying in the flat meadows. The wires also call to mind the stark steel high-tension towers which punctuate the same fields. Collection of the Newark Museum. Courtesy: Willard Gallery.

Kenneth Snelson chose highly polished steel wire to suggest the precision and symmetry of the Atom (1964, 27" x 12" x 12"). Courtesy: John Weber Gallery.

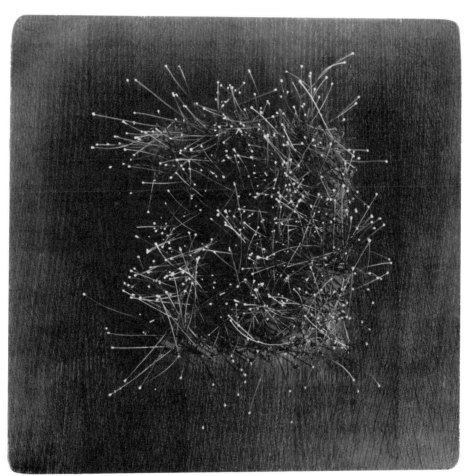

Pol Bury's Pointe Blancs (1966, 15 5/8" x 15 5/8") teases the viewer. Invisible motors cause the wires to move almost imperceptibly, making us wonder whether they do move, or whether we are seeing things. Courtesy: Lefebre Gallery.

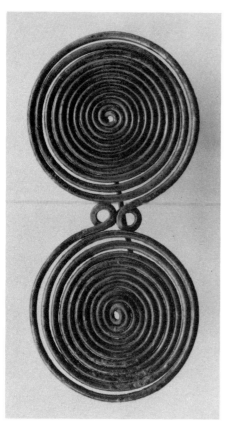

This bronze fibula originated in Greece, 10th–8th century B.C. The double-coil design remains popular today. Courtesy: The Metropolitan Museum of Art, Fletcher Fund, 1937.

A Ghanian gold necklace made through the lost-wax casting process using wax wires. Courtesy: The Museum of Primitive Art, New York.

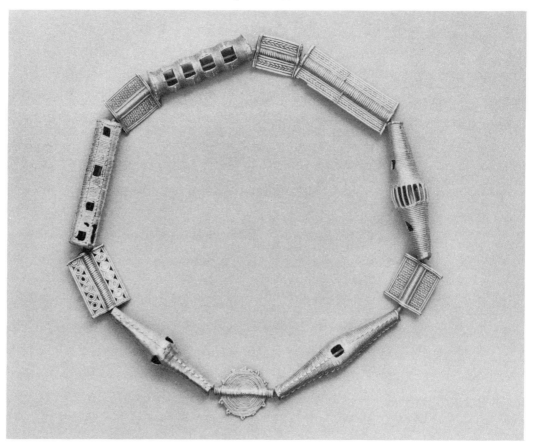

A Peruvian nose ornament (4 3/8″ wide) executed A.D. 200–300. The gold wires were worked directly. Courtesy: The Museum of Primitive Art. Photograph by Charles Uht.

Silver fork made during the 17th century, handle inlaid with silver wire. Courtesy: Museum of Decorative Art, Copenhagen.

Jadau work, in which semiprecious stones are held in place by wire and wire bezels, is still done today in Nepal. This silver-gilt 19th-century icon depicts Buddha. Courtesy: The Metropolitan Museum of Art.

Mary Lee Hu's Bird (1969, 4 1/2″ high), woven and wrapped fine silver wire. Courtesy: Mary Lee Hu.

A crystalline cloud of wire cells by Robert Leibel. Courtesy: Robert Leibel.

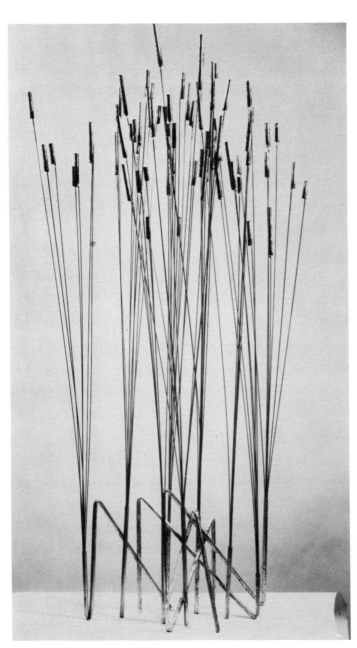

Cattails, by William Bowie, is a production piece that takes advantage of wire's consistency to execute many similar pieces in editions. Courtesy: William Bowie.

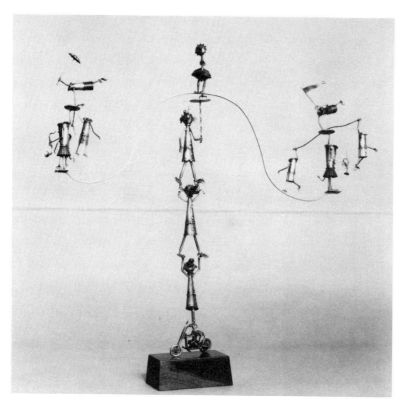

Earl Krentzin uses precious wires to suspend his cast silver and gold Balancers (23 1/2" high). Courtesy: Kennedy Galleries.

Olive and Black (1966, 61 1/2" x 42 1/4" x 12 1/2"), by Jesus Rafael Soto, shows the use of fine metal rods in combination with a graphic background. He teases our perceptions by combining moving and static linear elements. Courtesy: The Museum of Modern Art.

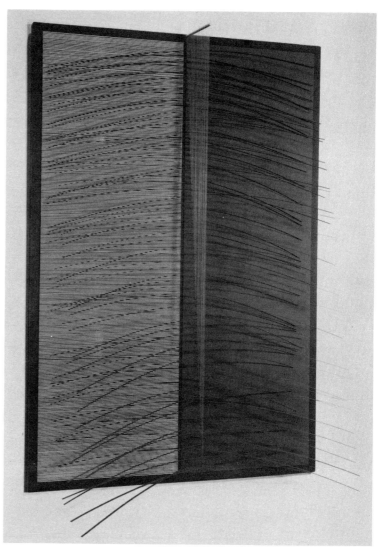

Cat Lamp (1928, 8 3/4" x 10 1/8" x 3 1/8"), by Alexander Calder, is constructed of a single piece of coiled, twisted, and bent wire. Though the material is basic the form has a pleasant feline. Courtesy: The Museum of Modern Art.

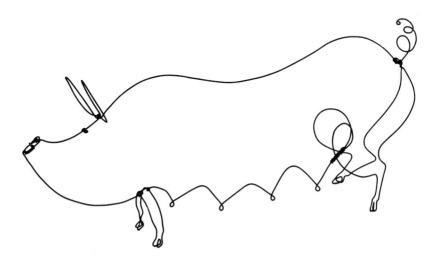

Calder's Sow (1928, 7 1/2" x 17"), again of a single piece of wire, proves that sculpture need not be udderly lifelike to be convincing. Courtesy: The Museum of Modern Art.

An Egyptian silver armlet of the Ptolemaic period (332–300 B.C.) reminds contemporary artisans that their craft is an ancient one. Courtesy: The Metropolitan Museum of Art.

Thomas Markusen hot-forges iron to achieve these flowing lines. Courtesy: Thomas Markusen.

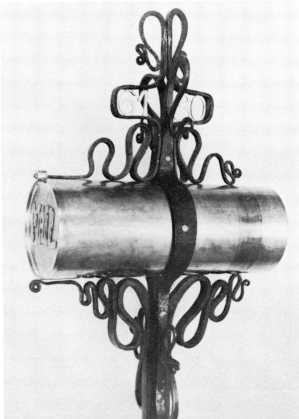

The Mexicans are masters of wirework armatures which are covered judiciously with papier-maché.

Constructed of clockwork parts, brass screening, and wire, Günther Haese's Caravan (1965, 11 1/8" x 15 1/2" x 11 1/2") evokes the image of a mechanistic convoy. Haese's use of wires in outline and screening to create the illusion of mass is especially effective. Courtesy: The Museum of Modern Art.

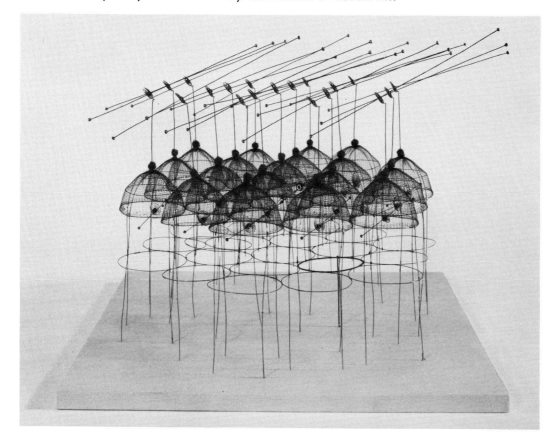

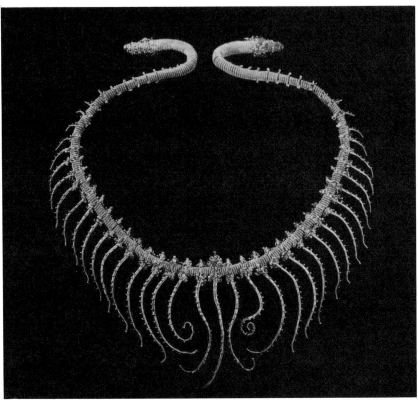

Neckpiece #3 (1968, 9″ x 10″), by Mary Lee Hu, is built of
fine and sterling wires wrapped on and around themselves.
Courtesy: Mary Lee Hu.

Laszlo Moholy-Nagy passes glass-headed wire pins through painted zinc screening
to create Space Modulator L13 (1936, 17 1/4″ x 19 1/8″). Courtesy: The Museum
of Modern Art.

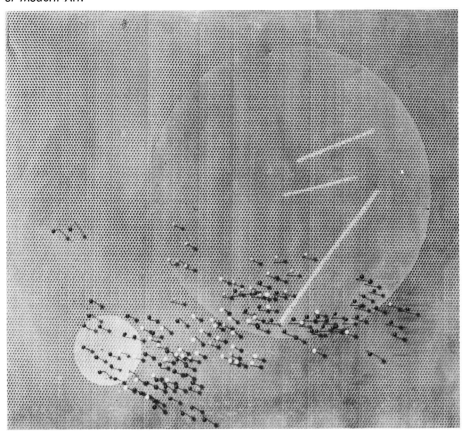

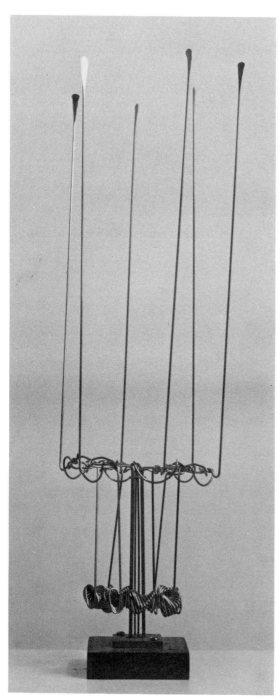

George Rickey bent, twisted, and forged stainless steel wire
in this stabile, Column of Six Lines with Spirals (1972, 18 1/2"
x 5"). Courtesy: George Rickey.

Dusan Dzamonja welds wire nails to create coarse, tense forms. Metal Sculpture 14 (1960). Courtesy: The Tate Gallery.

Resistors, transistors, capacitors, and stray strands were combined with pride. Courtesy: Honeywell.

Sculpture on the Sipplinger Berg (1972–73, 33′ x 12′ x 12′), by Matschinsky-Denninghoff. Flowing volumes created by welding hundreds of fine steel tubes together. Courtesy: Matschinsky-Denninghoff.

Chapter 2

A WIRE
VOCABULARY

WIRE CHARACTERISTICS

Wires are metals. As metals they have distinct characteristics. Among these specific properties are hardness, malleability, ductility, tensile strength, compression, shear, toughness, elasticity, torsion, brittleness, impact resistance, and rigidity. Each attribute varies according to the metal, and knowledge of how the different metal wires respond to more or less standardized tests meant to measure those qualities helps to determine which wires will be best suited to specific applications.

Wires are available in many different metals and many different diameters. A common form of packaging is the spool. Brass and copper wires, extremely workable materials, are relatively inexpensive and, because of this, are readily suited to experimentation.

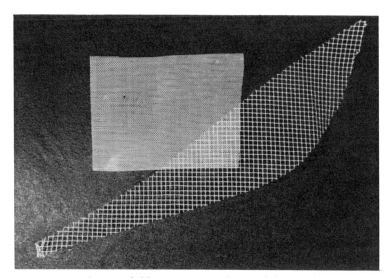

Wires are also available in processed and fabricated forms like carpenter's cloth and screening. Screening is most often made of steel, aluminum, copper, iron, or brass wire. The gauge and the density of the weave can vary greatly.

Hardness tells us something about the surface qualities of a metal. How easily will it scratch? How easily will it be dented or pitted? These are valuable things to know. A scientist named Friedrich Mohs developed a hardness scale that rates metals according to their relative abilities to withstand scratching by other metals. More precise grading systems have been developed as well.

Malleability relates to metal's ability to be beaten flat without splitting or cracking. Malleability becomes important in forging wires, where the goal is to extend the surface area without causing the metal to break apart. Gold remains the most malleable of metals; it may be beaten into a foil

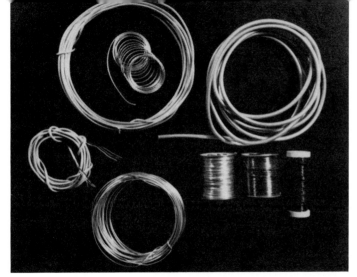

Choose wires for specific applications based on their individual qualities. Iron binding wire and soft precoated copper wires allow for fine work; insulated copper wires are often colorful; aluminum armature wires provide excellent structural support and good working qualities.

Several feet of telephone cable may provide weeks' worth of working material. Dozens of strands may be revealed when the outer layer of insulation is removed; they may be used insulated or used stripped of their colorful insulation to reveal a uniform copper hue.

five millionths of an inch thick. Some metals, such as the hard steel used in precision tools and dies, are not at all malleable. All wires are malleable,

Wires arranged in descending order of:	
Malleability	Ductility
Gold	Gold
Silver	Silver
Aluminum	Platinum
Copper	Iron
Tin	Copper
Platinum	Aluminum
Lead	Zinc
Zinc	Tin
Iron	Lead

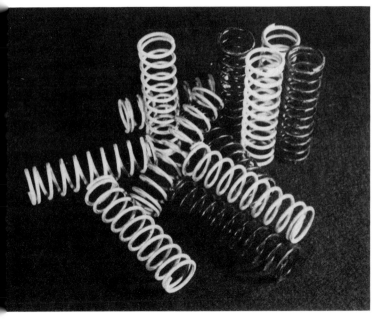

While some forms of wire are quite expensive, many of the most useful and usable wires are available for the asking. Coat hangers exemplify this notion—in an age of ecological concern, what better way to recycle them? The same holds true for wires from old electrical appliances. Wire forms such as springs may be combined with other wires as well. Do not attempt to unwind spring wire, however—it is difficult and dangerous.

Wires find application in nearly every aspect of modern life. In the kitchen, whisks and strainers make frequent use of wire.

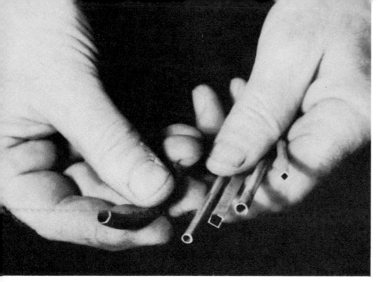

Besides traditional wire forms, there are the near-wires, the wirelike materials that are often used in combination with or in substitution for wire. Most notable of these are the metal tubes. These tubes, most often extruded while the metal is molten, come in as many shapes as wires do. Metal rods may be considered in this near-wire class as well. Artists such as the Matschinsky-Denninghoffs often begin with maquettes of wire and progress, on a monumental scale, to welded steel tubes. Tubes, much lighter than solid wires or rods, provide greater strength per unit of weight.

however. The order of malleability, from most to least, runs: gold, silver, aluminum, copper, tin, platinum, lead, zinc, iron.

Ductility relates to a metal's ability to be drawn into wire. The more ductile a metal, the more finely it may be drawn. Ductility and malleability are roughly related. Gold is the most ductile of metals as well as the most malleable. In descending order of ductility, other common metals are: silver, platinum, iron, copper, aluminum, zinc, tin, lead.

Tensile strength is the measure of the longitudinal stress that a metal can withstand without snapping. The measuring apparatus usually pulls from both ends a sample of the wire being tested, all the while measuring the amount of force being exerted. That measurement, expressed in pounds per square inch or kilograms per square centimeter, must be considered in applications where wires will be put under stress. By way of comparison, copper has ten times the tensile strength of tin, and steel has from four to ten times the tensile strength of copper.

Tension, compression, and *shear* all relate to the strength of metals. Compression relates to the amount of metal that may be squeezed or compressed in volume before it begins to crack or break apart. Shear refers to the resistance metal offers to shearing actions (like metal-cutting shears).

Toughness describes a broad category encompassing yet other distinct characteristics. Resistance to the strain of twisting, bending, and shock are generally referred to under *toughness.* One measure of this is *elasticity,* metal's ability to recover its normal size after being compressed or stretched. Another measure is *torsion,* the ability to return to normal size after being

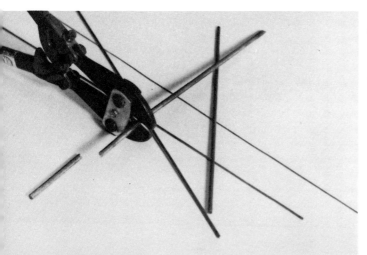

Wires may be cut in innumerable ways. Most craftsmen use metal shears or bolt cutters of some sort for rough cuts. Jewelers saw precious wires to obtain accurate, even, smooth ends. But thin wires may be snapped with scissors, nail nippers, or hands, and even thicker wires may be broken by bending them back and forth at a single point until fatigue causes the metal to snap. Though makeshift methods do service, a basic shears will be a worthwhile investment.

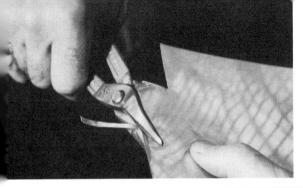

Flat wires may be made by cutting fine strips of metal from a sheet. It is also possible to create metal tubes by pulling flat wire through a drawplate until the sides meet, then soldering the edges together.

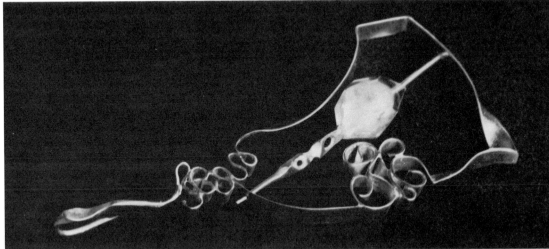

A flat wire hairpin by Maurice Abramson.

twisted. Still another measure is *brittleness*—how easily the metal snaps and fractures. Metals with high ductility and malleability are not **brittle**. For most wirework purposes, brittle metals are not useful. A further characteristic is *impact resistance,* ability to withstand sudden shocks.

A final quality of metals is *rigidity*—no mere euphemism for a lack of malleability. While flexibility and malleability are desirable qualities, many applications require that wires be rigid enough to accept and maintain shapes. It is often necessary to select rigid wires in applications where the wire will provide all structural support for the form. Increased rigidity can be effected by forging or drawing wires.

WIREDRAWING

Wiredrawing is one of the fundamental manufacturing and working processes available to the artisan. Wiredrawing was one of the earliest commercial techniques developed to manufacture wires and is still used today. Craftsmen frequently use this process to increase the rigidity of wire, or to reduce its diameter, or to change its shape.

Drawplates are hard steel or steel and diamond dies. They usually consist of a single piece of metal with series of tapered holes passing through them. The holes may be of considerably different shapes, including round, oval, square, triangular, hexagonal, octagonal, half-round, half-oval. In any series, however, the holes will be of the same geometric shape, successively decreasing in size.

To use the drawplate, first check all the holes to be used. Make certain that each is clean of all foreign matter. A lubricant, necessary to assure the smooth passage of wire, may be placed in the holes, or, in the case of a lubricant like beeswax, applied to the wire itself. Taper the end of the wire by filing, grinding, or hammering so that it will fit through one hole in the series. Enough should protrude from the other side of the plate so that it may be gripped securely by the drawtongs. Choose the first hole that resists easy passage of the wire.

Brown & Sharpe Gauge

Gauge	Inches Thick	Gauge	Inches Thick
1	.289	21	.028
2	.257	22	.025
3	.229	23	.022
4	.204	24	.020
5	.181	25	.018
6	.162	26	.016
7	.144	27	.014
8	.128	28	.013
9	.114	29	.011
10	.102	30	.010
11	.091	31	.009
12	.081	32	.008
13	.072	33	.007
14	.064	34	.006
15	.057	35	.006−
16	.051	36	.005
17	.045	37	.004+
18	.040	38	.004
19	.036	39	.004−
20	.032	40	.003

The Brown & Sharpe Gauge is a broadly used standardized measure of wire diameter.

Before drawing, one end of the wire must be filed so that it will fit through the drawplate. Taper about one and a half inches of wire so that the drawtongs may grip it securely. Rub beeswax along the wire to lubricate and ease passage through the plate. The wire should then be passed into the first hole through which it will not move easily.

Cross Sections of Round, Square, and Flat Wires

B & S* Gauge	Cross Section
9	●
12	●
16	●
18	●
20	●
24	·
8	■
12	■
14	■
18	▪
4 × 16	▬
6 × 18	▬
8 × 22	▬
* Brown & Sharpe	

Gripping the wire's tapered end with the drawtongs, pull the wire through in a continuous motion. Wire should always be drawn so that it emerges perpendicular to the drawplate. Repeat this process, drawing through successively smaller holes, skipping none, until the necessary diameter of wire is achieved. Generally, draw a length of wire that may be pulled through in one continuous motion (stops and starts create kinks in the wire).

Different shapes can be achieved by experimenting with the drawplate. Doubled strands of wire, for example, produce half-round wires when drawn through the round hole together. And twisted wire strands are often drawn and separated for use in filigree work. Consider the possibilities of drawing

A Joubert drawplate is set tightly in a vise on a sturdy table or bench. This is a plate for round wire. There are forty holes —each representing a different gauge of wire. Wire should always be drawn through these holes consecutively—never skipping a hole; wiredrawing is meant to be a gradual process; the more evenly and consistently the process is carried out, the less stress placed on the wire. The drawtongs at left traditionally have one curved handle to facilitate gripping and pulling wire.

After gripping the tapered wire end securely, pull the wire through in a clean smooth motion. The wire should emerge perpendicular to the drawplate. After each draw, test the wire. If it has become too stiff it may be annealed to restore original pliancy. If the wire is not annealed it may crack and break from the stress. Wire drawing, after all, is a compression process, and annealing releases the stress caused by forcing wire through an opening smaller than its own diameter.

different wires and combinations of wire through holes of different shapes—twisted or straight wires through ovular, square, and rectangular plates.

These combinations and experiments should not damage the drawplate. Although it is a precision instrument, it is meant for these purposes. Care should be exercised to make certain that it is clean before and after use. Also be certain never to allow wet wires or water to rust the steel. Like most fine tools, the drawplate will last many years with judicious use and minor attention.

Drawing wire makes it more rigid. The process compresses the metal. This quality is often desirable, especially when the craftsman wants fine wires to stand erect. As often, craftsmen want to reduce the wire's diameter, but want to maintain its flexibility and malleability.

ANNEALING

Annealing restores the original pliancy of metals. It is essentially a heating process, used on lengths of wire that have been drawn or on forms that have been hardened by cold forging or excessive shaping.

To anneal a length of wire, coil the wire gently and tuck the ends into the coil so that they do not melt. If possible, wrap the coil with a piece of the same wire. (Otherwise wrap with binding wire. The binding wire, however, must be removed before pickling or cooling in water.) To anneal, place the coil or worked forms on a charcoal block or asbestos sheet (at least ¼" thick) or over a wire mesh. For worked wires, annealing is necessary when the metal no longer responds to the working technique. Extreme rigidity and brittleness signal the need for annealing.

The one danger of annealing is overheating. The proper annealing temperature is usually far short of the melting point of the metal. But, since it is usually not possible for the craftsman to directly measure the temperature of the wire being annealed, shorthand devices are substituted. Anneal in a dark room, since the color changes of metal can be utilized as an indicator of the temperature. When the metal is red hot, remove heat. The most effective technique for estimating temperature may be to paint the form entirely with a flux that liquefies at approximately the proper annealing temperature. Flux will also prevent excessive oxidation caused by the heat.

Annealing may be accomplished with torch or kilns with temperature regulators. To anneal with a propane torch, use a large soft flame. Play the flame evenly over the entire surface of the piece or coil.

For kiln annealing, heat the kiln to annealing temperature and place the wire in the kiln on a support of wire mesh or ceramic kiln ware. Watch the metal carefully to be certain that it does not overheat.

Some wires may be allowed to air-cool, but others must be quenched in water or pickling solution immediately or they will simply not remain soft. Since it is difficult, without special information, to determine which wires require the pickling treatment, it is easier to just quench everything immediately. Wire may be held under running water with tongs, or it may be dropped gently into a pickling solution (discussed in Chapter 3). The pickling, which is a dilute acid bath, cools and cleans simultaneously.

Metal	Annealing Temperature (degrees Fahrenheit)	Melting Point (degrees Fahrenheit)
Aluminum	640–670	1220
Copper	700–1200	1981
Brass	800–1350	1680
Pure Gold	Annealing not necessary	1945
Gold Alloys	1200–1300	1945
Fine Silver	572	1760
Sterling Silver	1200	1760

TOOLS

Wireworking requires few specialized tools. For many shaping operations, hand manipulation works best. More precise bending work, of course, demands pliers of different sorts. In certain applications fine needle-nosed pliers will work best; for other purposes, however, broad flat-nosed instruments may be more useful. The tool depends upon the goal. Avoid pliers with toothed jaws if visible marks will harm the structure or design. If no smooth pliers are available, simply wrap surgical tape around each jaw to cover the teeth.

Many commercial jigs are available to form wire, to bend wire, and even to twist it. Some are very useful and save time, and the inexpensive ones can even save money. But most craftsmen find that their own jigs often become prized tools. Nails driven into wood blocks serve to define intricate forms. Dowels of different diameters may become the bases for coils. Jewelry mandrels are certainly effective but, if they are not readily at hand, tin cans and makeshift forms may be employed. In wirework, makeshift is definitely not merely "make-do".

Cutting some wires will require an investment in good shears. In particular, piano wires and other heavier wires like coat hanger wire, cannot be readily used unless they can be cut handily. Thinner copper and brass wires may be cut with an old pair of nail nippers. Again, sophistication will never be measured by tools, and what works well for individual artisans is always respected as a sufficient justification for nearly any technique—short of those involving unnecessary dangers.

As the various specific tools come into use in this book, their applications will be discussed in the text.

INDIVIDUAL METALS

A brief discussion of the metal wires most commonly used by artisans follows. These brief characterizations only generally explain the origin, properties, and working limitations of the individual wires. Firsthand experience and further reading will help to develop expertise in any of the materials discussed below.

Gold

Gold and copper are probably the earliest metals known to man, because they are among the few metals found in flake, grain, or nugget form. The earliest gold was probably panned or picked from riverbeds; today it is also separated from ores by a variety of other processes including amalgamation, cyanidation, and smelting.

Gold has been a prized substance for centuries. Its brilliant yellow color, and the fact that it resists oxidation and retains that color, no doubt contributed to this popularity. More significant for the artisan is the fact that gold is the most ductile and the most malleable of all metals. For this reason goldwork may be much finer than any other.

Gold wire is available in many shapes, including round, half-round, square, rectangular, and some special shapes as well. The variety is so great that, when ordering, one must specify karat, color, length, weight, and gauge of wire.

Gold Alloys

Pure gold is used rarely in applications where substantial wear will occur. It is exceptionally soft, denting and marring easily. For that reason, various alloys of gold and other metals have been developed. Each alloy has characteristics of its own.

White gold, one such alloy, consists of 25 percent platinum or 12 percent palladium plus gold. Its melting point is higher than that of pure gold and it is tougher. White gold must be worked very evenly, otherwise it will crack during annealing or during later work. *Green gold* contains 35 percent silver or silver with the addition of cadmium and zinc. Green gold is soft and can be worked easily. *Yellow gold,* a most versatile alloy, is a combination of gold, silver, and copper. The copper lends a reddish tint. Working qualities of gold-copper alloys will vary with the percentage of copper.

Most gold wire is alloyed, but it is not referred to as an alloy; rather, the percentage of gold is tacitly recognized through the karat number. Twenty-four-karat gold, for example, is 100 percent gold. Twelve-karat gold is 50 percent gold, and so on. Wires are also available as *gold-filled*; these consist of a thin layer of gold over another metal.

Gold Solders

Gold solders are available in many temperatures and in many colors—to match the cast of different alloys. Solders of 18k, 14k, and 10k are readily available. As a rule of thumb, craftsmen use a gold solder of lower karat than the gold being soldered, but one still must be certain that the melting-flowing points of the solder are lower than the melting point of the gold.

Choosing and Working Gold Wire

The choice of color and karat of gold will always depend upon the application. Softness and rigidity may determine whether a lower or higher karat will be necessary. If the gold will be used in combination with other materials, the color may be of importance. And technical considerations may play in the decision as well. Gold-zinc alloys, for example, are unsuitable for enameling. Finally, the relative expense of higher karat golds may outweigh smaller advantages.

Otherwise, gold is suitable for all wireworking techniques. It may be formed and forged, soldered and annealed. Special care should be given to soldering and annealing operations. Because gold is precious, it is wise to use progressive solderings (see Chapter 3), beginning with the hardest solder and progressing to the easiest in order to protect joints previously attached. Use the fluxes designed for gold and, when prolonged heat will be necessary, apply a thicker paste flux to protect the metal from oxidation.

Overheated gold will collapse, and overheating may also bring the alloys to the surface, making cleaning very difficult. Annealing, therefore, demands special care. Green, yellow, and red golds require heating to approximately 1220° F, or a dull reddish glow, in order to soften them properly. White gold demands the slightly higher temperature of 1400° F. Quench red gold in water or pickling solution while it is hot. Other golds may be cooled in the solution or allowed to cool naturally. A fine technique of determining the temperature is to apply a flux that liquefies in the proper range. This provides the best clue to estimating metal heat.

Silver

Silver, too, is found pure in its natural state but, more often, silver results from the refining process—a by-product of gold, zinc, lead, and copper ores.

Pure silver offers the same qualities as gold does; in fact, it is second only to gold in malleability and ductility. Today, silver's brilliance and resistance to corrosion make it a desirable and practical substance with which to work.

Silver Alloys

Like gold, silver is too soft to be used for most objects in its pure state. *Fine silver,* 999.0 parts per thousand silver, and *high fine silver,* 999.5 parts silver, are available and are valued in certain applications. Mary Lee Hu, for instance, executes crochetlike forms in fine silver. Its softness allows her to manipulate it intricately, and, when formed, the structure gives the soft silver enough support to make its use practical as well as technically successful.

Silver is not generally alloyed. In the United States, metals containing less than 90 percent silver may not even be called silver. The most common alloy, *sterling silver,* consists of 925 parts silver and 75 parts copper. Even though alloys of silver are not used in jewelry, combinations are used in industry and for coinage and dentistry.

Sterling and fine-silver wires may be purchased readily. Silver wires are available as flat, round, half-round, oval, half-oval, triangular, hexagonal, ball wire, half-ball wire, bead wire, fine, and sterling bezel wires. All wires are sold by Brown & Sharpe gauge, a standard measure of diameter that also corresponds to sheet-metal thicknesses. Most silver and gold wires are sold in annealed or soft forms, unless a specific request is made for nonannealed wires.

Silver tubings are also readily available in square, rectangular, and round configurations of different dimensions. Tubings are also catalogued according to the Brown & Sharpe (B & S) scale.

Using and Working Silver Wire

Silver may be worked in all methods. As with gold, care must be taken in the annealing process in order not to destroy the metal. Silver should be heated to 1100–1200°F. Anneal it properly; it may then be hot quenched or allowed to cool in the air. Overheating should be avoided since it causes the formation of a *fire scale.* The fire scale is a copper oxide formation resulting from change in the molecular composition of the metal due to the overheating. The oxide can be removed by placing the wire in a cold bath of 50 percent nitric acid and 50 percent water. Remove the metal as soon as the fire-scaled areas turn black and the rest of the silver turns grey; wash the form in running water. For stubborn areas repeat the process. Better yet, heat the silver carefully so that the metal will not be weakened by such continuous subjection to acidulous cleaning solutions.

Silver may be colored or antiqued in the same manner as other metals. Such surface treatments are discussed later.

Copper

Conjecture has it that copper is the oldest metal known to man, discovered nearly ten thousand years ago in the valley of the Tigris and Euphrates rivers. Copper finds innumerable applications in crafts and industry. Because of its high electrical conductivity copper wires are most commonly used in electrical appliances.

For the artisan, copper is *the* original metal. Copper allowed and begat the development of nearly every metalworking technique known today. Little wonder, then, that copper finds widespread use alone or in combination with other metals and other media, too.

Form copper wire in any manner. In soldering copper, silver solders and fluxes should usually be used and, as in any soldering operation, care should be taken to avoid the excessive application of heat.

Copper wires harden if overworked. When such increased rigidity is not desired, anneal the copper at 700–1200°F to restore flexibility and softness to the metal.

A large number of copper-based alloys are available in wire form, including metals with zinc, nickel, silver, and aluminum content.

Copper wires come in a wide range of gauges, from the filamentous strands used in electrical applications to thick copper rods. Drawplates, available with holes in a wide variety of shapes, can produce exciting effects with copper wire.

Brass

The most important copper alloy is brass. It consists of copper and zinc. There are essentially two classes of brasses—the *alpha* group, containing 36 percent or less of zinc, and the *beta* group, containing 37 percent or more of zinc. The alpha group works very well cold, but the beta brasses should be worked hot. Different brasses have different annealing temperatures. Those most often used in jewelry work, however, soften at approximately 1620–1650°F.

Aluminum

Aluminum is a recent discovery. Only with the advent of inexpensive refinement techniques in this century has it become readily available.

Aluminum's sterling qualities include extreme lightness, high malleability, and corrosion resistance. Because it is so very light and flexible, even relatively thick aluminum wires may be formed with ease. And aluminum wires are especially responsive to forging.

Most often, it seems, aluminum wires are thought of as structural elements. Sculptors often use aluminum to create the armatures for large sculptures, only rarely using aluminum as the sculptures themselves. There is no reason that aluminum should not be used directly and for itself more often. The metal will accept a high gloss, and it readily accepts surface treatments that affect the metal or are applied to it.

Soldering Aluminum

Soldering aluminum wires requires more skill and patience than with other metal wires. Alcoa makes a series of solders and fluxes for different grades of aluminum, and these are highly recommended. The primary difficulty with aluminum soldering is breaking through the thin oxide layer that develops so quickly (and becomes so impervious). The oxides must be removed to create a solid bond; scraping with steel wool and wire brushes helps, as does abrasion during soldering by reaching under the molten solder with a pointer or scraper. Another helpful technique is to apply solder to the ends of aluminum wire to be joined, allow the solder to harden, and then join the solders, possibly with the addition of more solder.

CLEANING AND POLISHING

Metal wires are resilient and, though they may become dirty and tarnished through use or working, most can be cleaned and polished easily. A pickling solution of one part sulphuric acid to ten parts water—or a non-acidic cleaner like Sparex[R]—is used after all heating, annealing, and soldering operations. That same solution may be used to clean metals at other times. Only be careful to rinse the wire in running water afterward, and always dry metals carefully to prevent further corrosion. (See Chapter 3 for more on pickling.)

Because many wire compositions are somewhat delicate, the more powerful polishing tools should be avoided. Usually, a high luster may be achieved by using a wire brush, steel wool, emery buffs, an abrasive cloth, fine sandpaper, or a wire brush attached to a hand or flexible-shaft drill.

Those materials serve to clean and polish at the same time. Some do leave rougher surfaces than others, but in some instances it may be necessary to begin with a rougher polisher, such as heavy grit sandpaper, and progress to finer papers in order to achieve the proper finish. Most often the wires will require very little work, however, and buffing with steel wool should bring out a pleasant lustre. High shine will require the use of a wire brush on an electric drill, or rouge on a polishing cloth.

COLORING WIRES

Heat

All metals change color when exposed to heat. The duration of heating will usually determine the intensity of the color. Since each metal will react differently to prolonged heat exposure, experiment first. Apply low heat for long periods rather than high heat, since the lower temperatures present less risk of causing the wire to collapse. Metals are often textured, in a process called *reticulation,* by heating the surface, too.

Chemical

A variety of chemical colorings are possible as well. The most commonly used chemicals for this purpose are liver of sulphur, copper sulphate, copper nitrate, barium sulphide. These chemicals, alone or in combination with other chemicals, turn different metals different shades. Liver of sulphur, used on copper, silver, and gold, produces a brownish-black. Barium sulphide produces colors ranging from a gold tint (on silver) when used cold, to a blue-black when used hot. Copper sulphate necessarily produces different colors when used on copper, brass, or bronze. All these substances are sold in prediluted forms for immediate use, and all, too, are available in powder, cake, or concentrate with instructions for mixing with water. Experiments on scrap wire remain the best way to gauge and control coloring effects. A final note: Heating metals briefly on a hot plate or in an oven immediately after applying the chemical colorant often intensifies the color.

For best effect, always clean the wires before attempting to color them —grease invariably interferes with the reaction.

Acrylics

Space-age plastics cannot be forgotten either. Degreased wires readily accept acrylic colors. Use acrylics like paint. These paints are soluble in water, come in every color imaginable, and may be mixed together in many more unimaginable colors, too. A special quality of acrylics that is explored in Chapter 6 on wire as armature is their potential for adding dimension to basic forms. Acrylic colors mixed with acrylic gesso or modeling paste become an integral part of the structure when applied to or painted on wires. Though the color remains water soluble when wet, remember that, once it dries, the color becomes permanent.

THE VOCABULARY

As with any material, there are certain modes and means of working wire. This section details some of the basic goals, techniques, and products possible through combinations of different units of wire vocabulary.

Clumping

Short stumps of wire bound and clumped together can define areas. Pol Bury combines hundreds and thousands of fine strands of nylon wire. The ends are accentuated. The illusion of forested land, bunched buds, straw, and grass suggests that the use of clumped wires is successful in describing masses loosely.

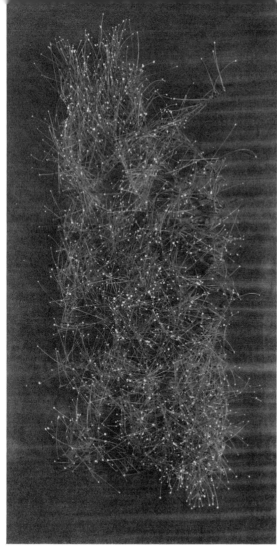

Pol Bury's 1914 White Points (1964; 39" x 20" x 5") utilizes short pieces of nylon wire. Truncated wires may be used to achieve staccato effects. Many wires, like those combined here by Bury, may be clumped and massed to create a sense of form and density. Collection: The Museum of Modern Art, Philip Johnson Fund.

Crumpling

Ignore for the moment the reasoned possibilities that wire offers. Crumple a piece. Crumple it again and again. Wrap and mold the wire into any shape you can think of. Try pressing the crumpled metal into a negative form—an ice cube tray, a glass, an eggshell. Spread the wire everywhere within the form, and allow it to spill over and beyond the boundaries imposed. Irrational crumpled wires can define volumes in different ways than can orderly attached wires.

What a surprise! Crumpled wrapped and balled wires will describe any volume they are forced into: witness the egg.

Bending

A single piece of wire will not stand by itself. Bent, the same strand will stand. Bent to form, it will describe an area.

Many wires are malleable enough to be bent by hand. To obtain sharp angles with any wire, however, use pliers or a jig, or the edge of a table. Experiment with two-dimensional forms: flat faces and curvilinear doodles.

Wire will define three-dimensional space in many ways. Norbert Kricke's early works with single strands make us imagine other forms—they outline and suggest limits and possible volumes. They represent changing forms that will vary continually as we pass around and through them. His later work suggests the possibilities for defining space with wires bent to echo each other. The wires follow and track each other, finally diverging, speeding past, or, perhaps, coalescing.

Bent wires may suggest forms and faces we are familiar with: Calder's wire portraits; cubes and other regular geometric forms.

The devices for bending wire will vary too. Jigs of nails and wood provide accurate and efficient bending models. Some more complex forms do require precise wooden molds.

Paper tubes, wooden dowels, metal rods, all serve as bases for wire coils. Triangular, square, or irregular forms can also be used in coiling. Tightly wrapped wire creates one type of coil. Stretched and twisted coils produce other results.

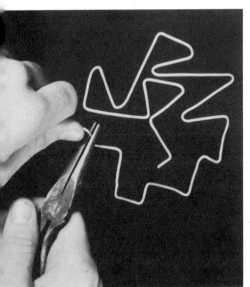

To achieve angular bends in wire, use a flat-nosed pliers. If tooth marks will mar the design, employ smooth-jawed tools or wrap those grinning jaws with pieces of surgical tape.

These two pins by Mitchell Egenberg were made entirely of brass wire bent to shape and forged slightly. The duckpin bowls us over.

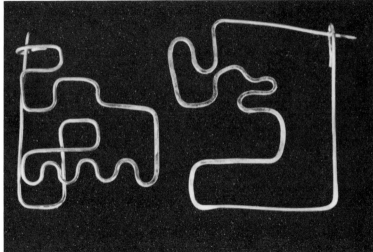

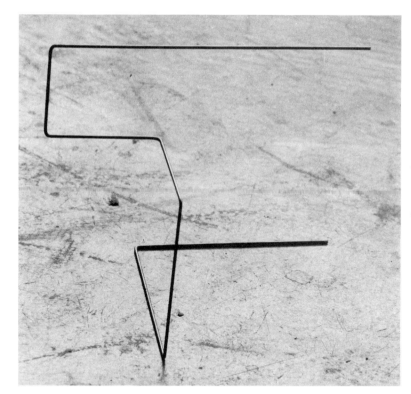

An early wire form of Norbert Kricke's entitled Raumplastik (1950), is a single piece of wire and six right angles. Courtesy: Norbert Kricke.

Raum-Zeit-Plastik Lutticher (1952, 18″ x 40″ x 13″), by Norbert Kricke, defines space without attempting to describe planes. Courtesy: Norbert Kricke.

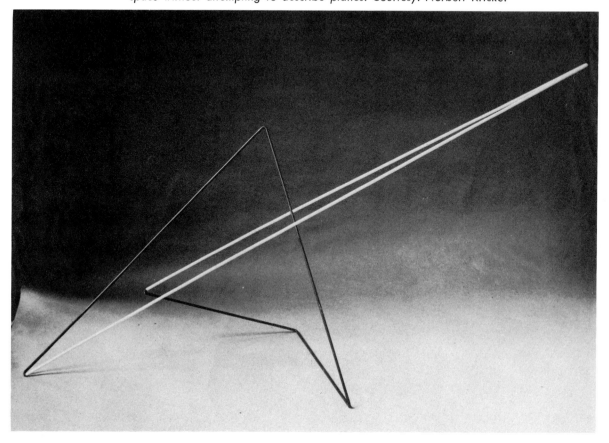

A Meander (1973, 9" x 3" x 12") stabile in steel wire by George Rickey. Rickey bends his forms precisely to achieve the accurate balance that allows the elements to float freely. Courtesy: George Rickey.

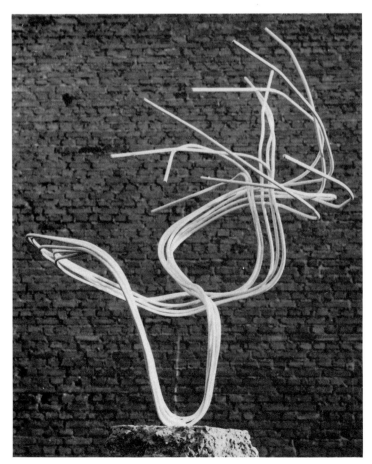

Here is a consideration of wire and density as suggested by Norbert Kricke's Raumplastik Wein (1955, 30" high), in which swirling wires echo one another closely until they diverge, spilling off into space. Courtesy: Norbert Kricke.

43

Aluminum armature wire may be bent into intricate shapes by hand because it is extremely light and flexible. The elements in this density study complement—but do not copy—one another.

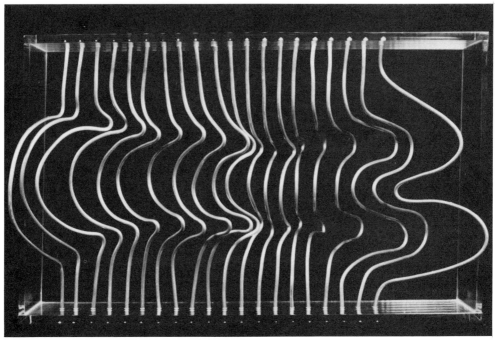

The series is combined in an acrylic frame.

Each wire may be turned, adjusted to vary the density of the image. In one view, twenty straight lines are all that viewer sees.

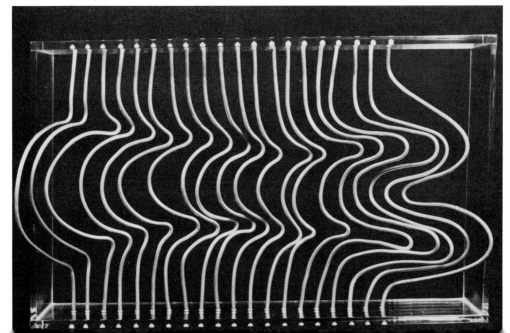

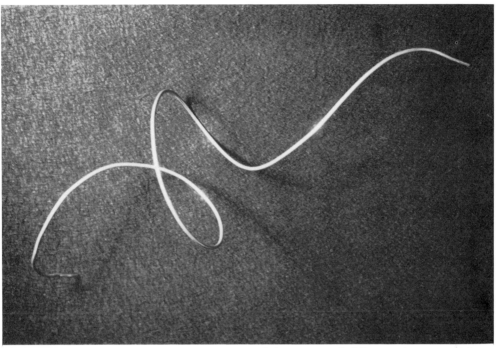

Bent wire can suggest movement, it can define areas of differing densities, and it can suggest volumes.

Different wires bent in different ways may suggest the combination or intersection of volumes as well.

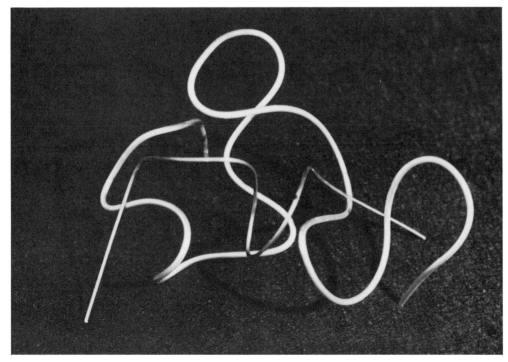

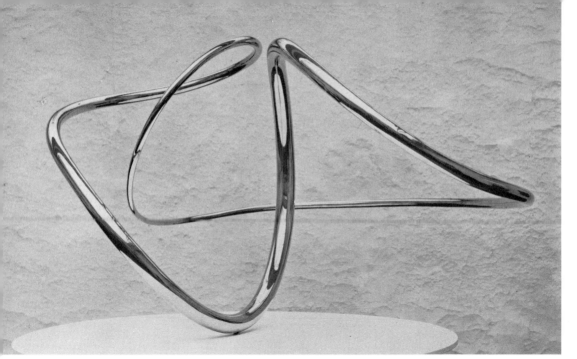

Brussels Construction (1958) of stainless steel by Jose de Rivera creates a feeling of moving volumes contained by the fine polished lines of the sculpture. Courtesy: Art Institute of Chicago.

Kricke's stainless steel sculpture of 1965 makes no pretense or attempt to define, describe, or analyze space. It is pure form, varying by angle of view and light. Courtesy: Norbert Kricke.

Wires may attempt to limit and contain and solidify actual volumes too. Alexander Calder's portrait of Marion Greenwood (1929–30, 12 5/8″ x 11″ x 11 3/8″) employs brass wire to caricature her features and the form— the very shape—of her head. Collection: The Museum of Modern Art.

Wire may be used to describe specific forms. Bent aluminum wire within a rectangular solid.

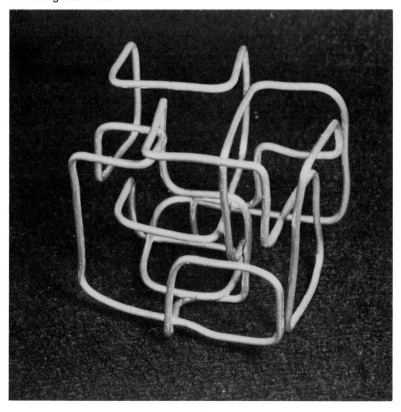

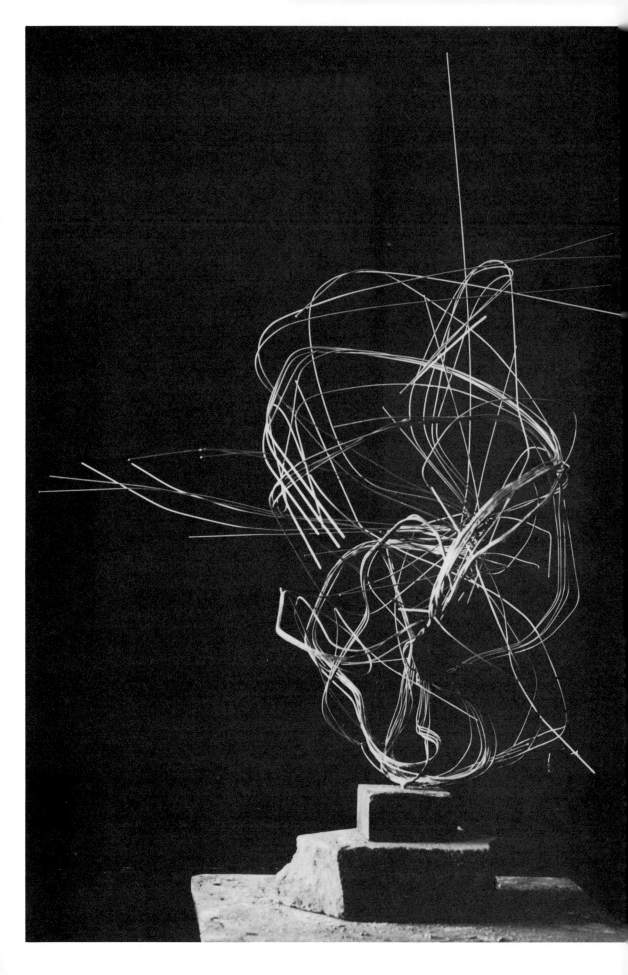

Wire may be bent by hand, with pliers, and with jigs. Jigs can be made by simply driving nails into a piece of wood. Attach an end of wire to one nail and begin wrapping.

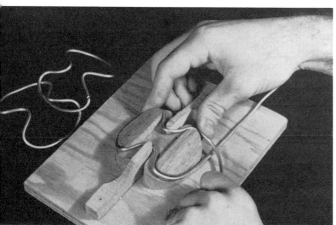

It may be difficult to approximate true curves with nails, so wooden jigs may better suit some shapes.

A series of interlocking curves was made in assembly-line fashion with the aid of the wooden jig.

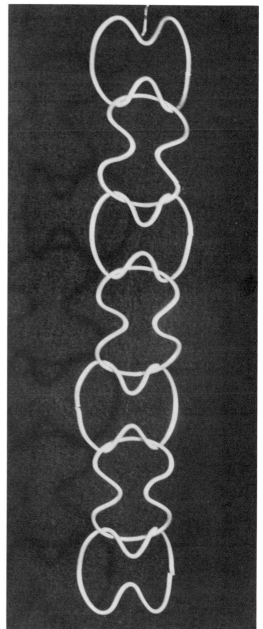

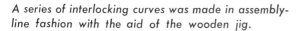

Norbert Kricke, Raumplastik 1961, stainless steel wire 18″ high. Courtesy: Norbert Kricke.

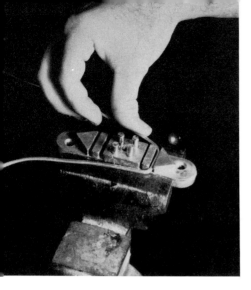

Commercial jigs are often helpful in bending right angles, certain acute angles, and loops, curves, and coils. This particular jig, of aluminum, comes with four removable steel pins. The channels in the jig are of different sizes; they accommodate most wires. This particular jig helps make 90°, 60°, 45°, and 30° bends.

The steel pins may be used in any combination to create tight loops and coils . . .

. . . or more open forms.

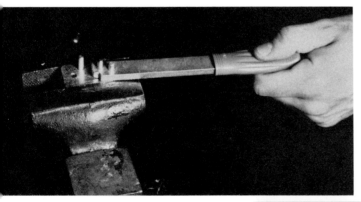

Another variety of wire bender employs a movable handle. Wire is fitted into place between steel pins and the handle is turned to bend the wire around a pivot. It's a handy gadget, and it also aids in making larger curves.

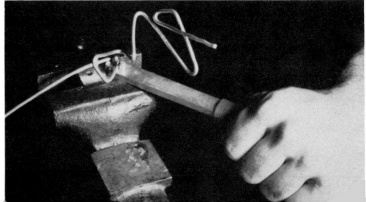

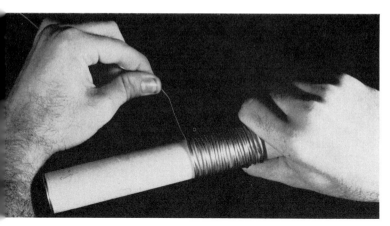

Coil wire by wrapping it around a tube.

A springlike wire coil is made by bending the ends around.

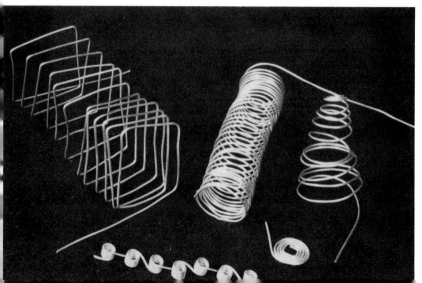

Coils may be made in many shapes: round, square, conical, and in succession.

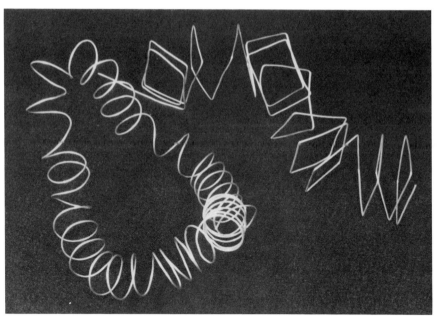

Coils may be modified by pulling, twisting, bending, and crushing.

Forging

Forging refers to the process of shaping wires by hammering them against a hard surface. Special stakes are tempered specifically for use as forging surfaces. Most often, however, an anvil, a vice top, or a steel block is used. Steel hammers of different shapes may be used to cold-forge wire. Always clean both the hammer and the hammering surfaces before and during forging to make certain that dirt and dust do not become imbedded in those surfaces. Marred and pitted surfaces will transfer the same texture to the wires, and in the more malleable and precious materials this is especially apparent and undesirable. Textures may be achieved by different beating approaches, but they should not be allowed to result accidentally or in a random fashion from imperfect tools.

Many effects can be achieved through forging. Metals may be compressed, but usually forgers attempt to expand and flatten and form the wire.

Begin by hammering the wire gradually. Since wires of different metals have different malleability, some will become too hard to work with sooner than others. When the hammer begins to bounce back without affecting the metal, the wire needs to be annealed. Annealing softens the wire, which may then be forged further. Eventually the wire will reach its limits and further forging will merely cause it to crack apart. With practice the craftsman can learn to work within those limits.

Certain hammers have rounded (ball peen) surfaces. They may be used to shape the wire, to raise and curve it. Rounded heads also allow the artisan to achieve different surface effects on the metal.

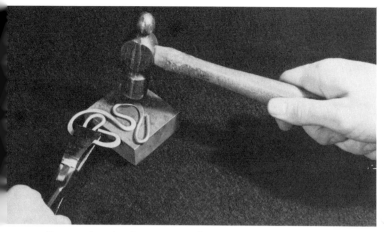

Forge wires by hammering them against an anvil or a steel block. Hammers are available in many shapes and sizes. Always be certain that the surfaces contacting the wire are smooth and clean. Marred and dirty anvils and hammer faces will transfer imperfections to the wire.

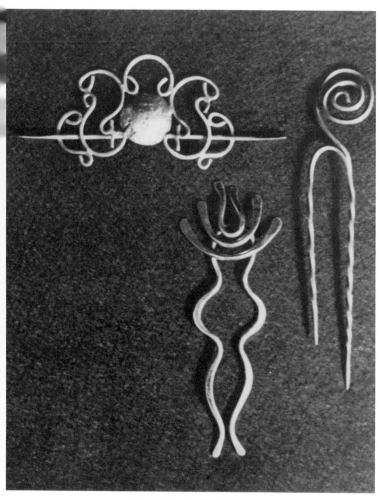

Forged wire hairpins.

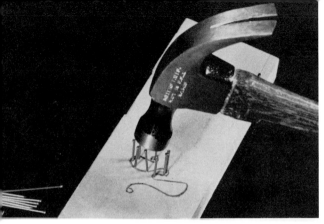

Forging is most often used in combination with other techniques—especially bending. Here a jig is being made to bend wire elements that will later be forged.

Intricate forms may be created, depending on the wire's malleability. Lift the bent element away from the nails carefully.

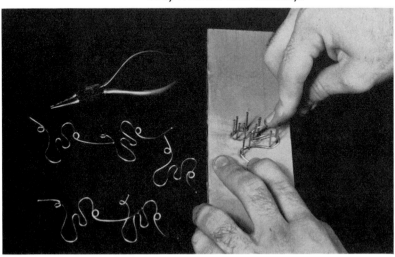

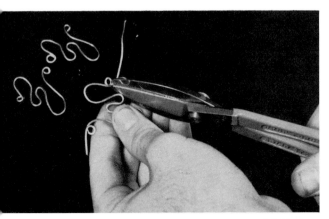

Unwanted ends of wire are snipped off.

Parts of each piece are flattened slightly.

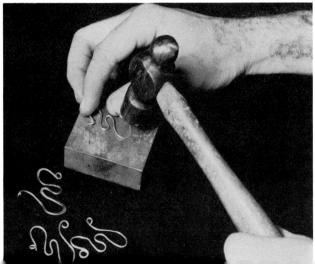

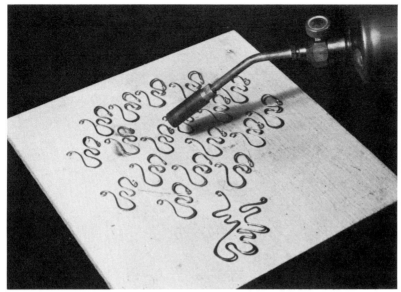

And every one is annealed to restore its original pliancy. Additional forging is now possible.

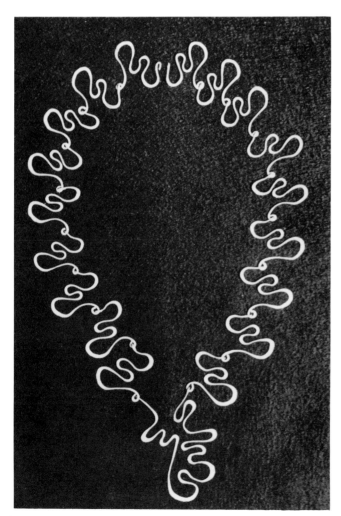

The final pieces are linked together.

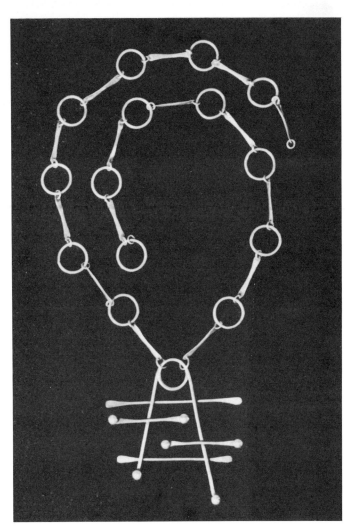

A bent and forged necklace by Mitchell Egenberg.

Bent and forged gold-wire neckpiece by E. R. Nele of Munich, Germany. Courtesy: Victoria and Albert Museum, London.

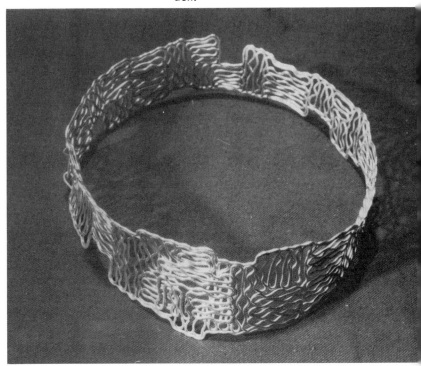

Bowl of soldered copper wire rings.

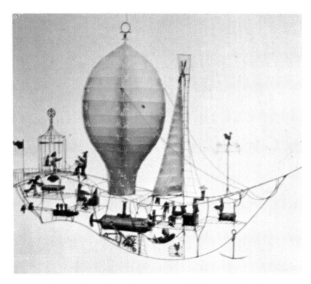

Sailing Ship #1 (1974), by Clifford Earl. Courtesy: Clifford Earl.

Neckpiece #15 (1974), by Mary Lee Hu. Fine silver, sterling, and precoated copper wires. Courtesy: Mary Lee Hu.

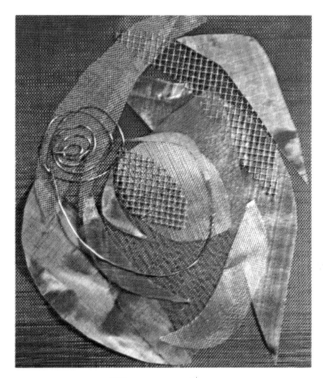

Wire screen collage.

Wrapped wire figure by Jay Hartley Newman.

Silver, gold, and copper cloisonné over copper by William Harper.

Gold filigree belt from Thailand.

Aluminum wire screening embroidered with insulated copper wire.

Pride of capacitors, transistors, and stray strands. Courtesy: Honeywell.

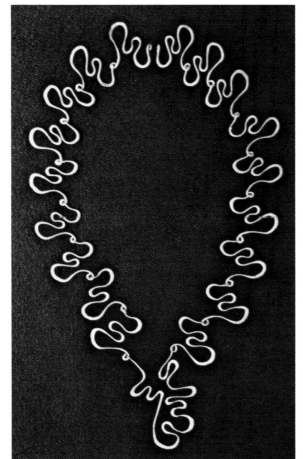

A forged brass necklace by Lee Scott Newman.

AF 210 (1972), a "compage" of wires and paper pulp, by Golda Lewis. Courtesy: Golda Lewis.

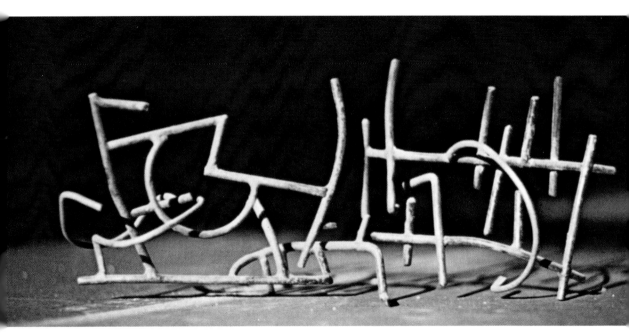

Interruption©, of iron wire, by Herbert A. Feuerlicht.

Mexican papier-mâché and wire bull.

Soldered wire geometric.

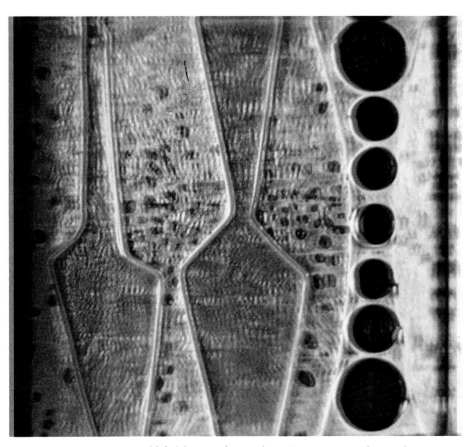

Cloisonné over gold foil by A. Alan Perkins. Courtesy: A. Alan Perkins.

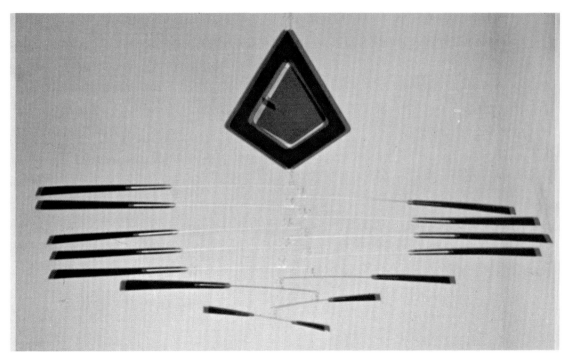

Steel wire and tin mobile by Robert R. Spooner. Courtesy: Robert R. Spooner.

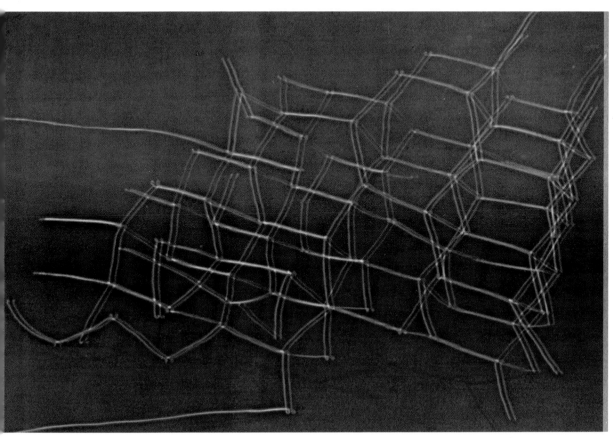

Smoke Revisited, four-junction wire sculpture by Robert Leibel. Courtesy: Robert Leibel.

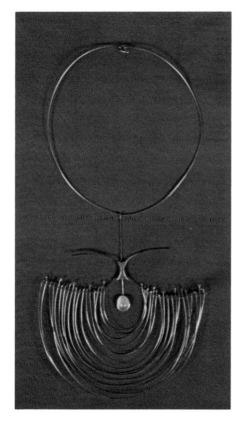

Gold wire necklace by John Snidecor.

Wax wire pin, cast in gold by Maurice Abramson.

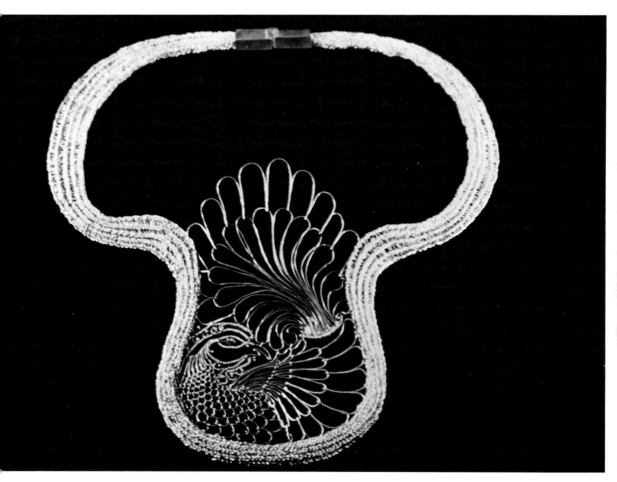

Neckpiece #13 (1974), fine silver, fine gold, and gold-filled brass wires, by Mary Lee Hu. Courtesy: Mary Lee Hu.

Twisting

Twisting is probably the most basic of wire attachment mechanisms. Like bending, we twist wires intuitively. But twisting can also be an aesthetic device.

Soft wires are readily twisted by hand. Elementary mechanical devices like vise and dowel provide one alternative for stiffer wires. A hand or power drill will provide a more mechanistic, quicker solution to the same problem of twisting stiff wires.

Wires need not be the same type or quality to be twisted together, nor need they be particularly long or short. Every sort and length may be twisted into something, for some purpose.

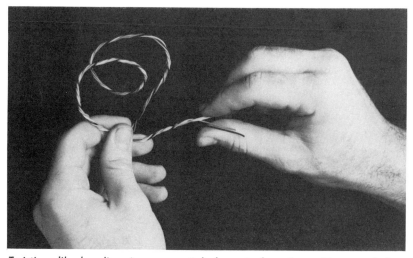

Twisting, like bending, is an essential element of a wireworking vocabulary. Many wires may be twisted by hand.

A variety of mechanical devices can make twisting easier. One method is to loop wires around a wooden dowel and secure the ends in a vise. The dowel supplies additional leverage.

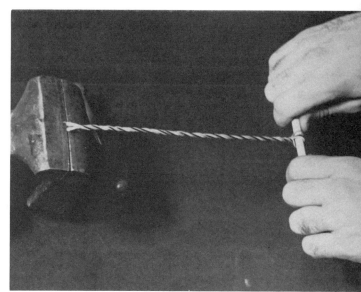

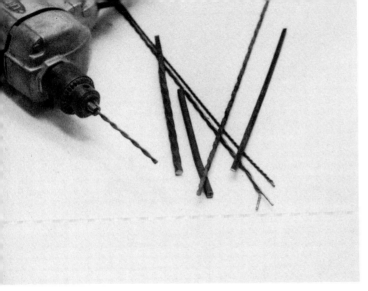

Clifford Earl twists thicker wires and rods with an electric hand drill.

Secure the wires in the jaws of the drill
. . .

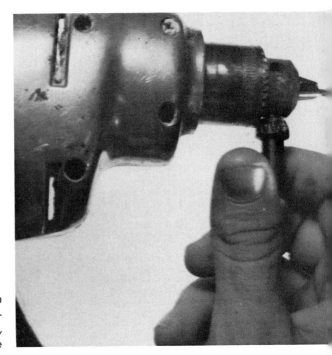

. . . secure the ends in a vise, and then turn on the drill in spurts. It is easy to over-twist wires when using an electric drill, but hand drills may be used in the same manner.

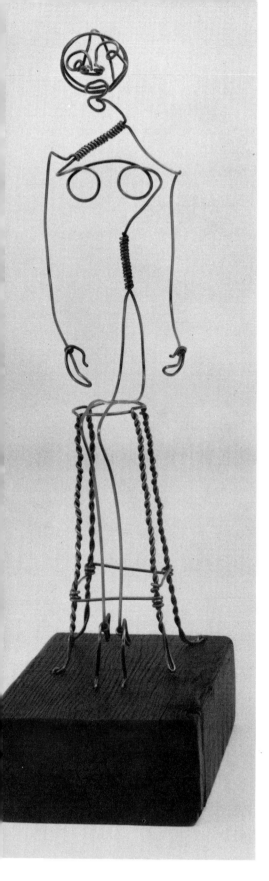

Alexander Calder's Soda Fountain (1928, 1 5/8"
x 5 1/2" x 3 1/2") employs the wire twist struc-
turally and aesthetically. Collection: The Museum
of Modern Art.

Another view of the Soda Fountain gives an important insight into the way wire outline sculpture
should work: from many angles. Because wire is
so flexible, and because we do not need to have
the entire form filled in order to imagine the
volume, wires should be shaped to be "read"
from many angles. Collection: The Museum of
Modern Art.

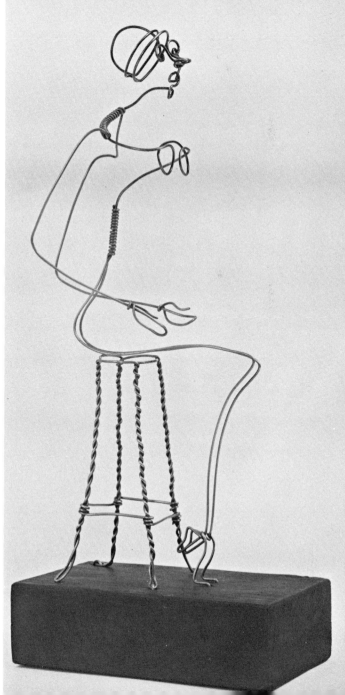

Braiding

Akin to twisting, the braiding process is no different from braiding hair or string. Simply hammer nails into a block of wood to provide a starting point and a working surface. Wrap the wire ends around the nails and begin.

Braids take many shapes and styles. Single, double, triple—innumerable—strand braids are possible. Fine wires may be braided around other stiffer forms. Stiffer wires complicate the process, so try to soften these by annealing. Or, consider using fine silver and fine gauge copper, each of which braids beautifully.

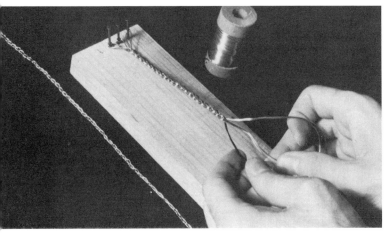

Wires may be braided in nearly any number, and in many patterns as well. A successful working aid is the nail block shown here. The wires must be pulled taut in order to braid evenly, and one way to provide the tension is to clamp the wood down to the table.

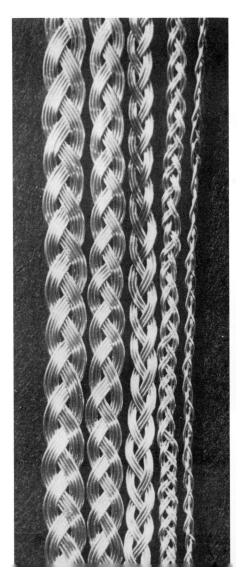

These copper wire braids suggest that the number of individual strands may be increased many, many times.

Fine wires may also be braided around other objects and materials. These filaments found application as decoration for a flexible metal hairband.

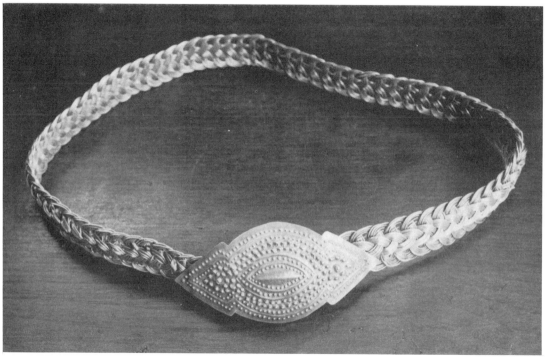

A multiple braiding technique was used in this antique Thai belt. It is made of an impure silver wire. Close-up of braid below.

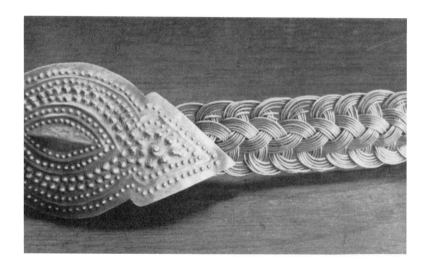

Comical toy animals can be made by braiding and weaving with insulated wire.

Crochet and Macramé

The crocheting of wire has been developed to a fine art by Mary Lee Hu. She always uses fine silver or fine gold or a very thin copper. Hu knows that stiffer wires simply are not flexible enough to be worked in this technique.

Every stitch should find translation into wire. Macramé and simple looping are extremely viable possibilities as well.

Mary Lee Hu crochets with fine silver wire. Because the fine silver is very soft, it may be looped and pulled through quite easily, but, unlike natural fibers, it will not find a consistent shape by itself. The craftsman must therefore be certain that every loop conforms to the proper pattern. Courtesy: Mary Lee Hu.

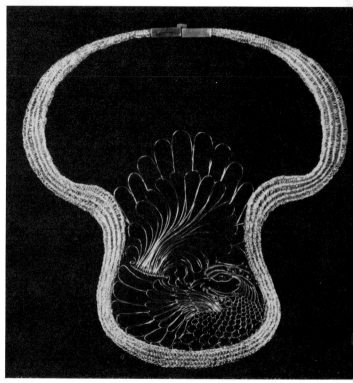

A crochetlike technique that Mary Lee Hu employs frequently is looping and bending. The center section of Neckpiece #13 (1974, 8" x 10") was made in this manner. The rows of loops are often of a continuous strand, but they need not be, because the wire may be wrapped and bent to shape—and will maintain that shape. The method is effective. This piece is of fine silver, fine gold, and gold-filled brass wires. Courtesy: Mary Lee Hu.

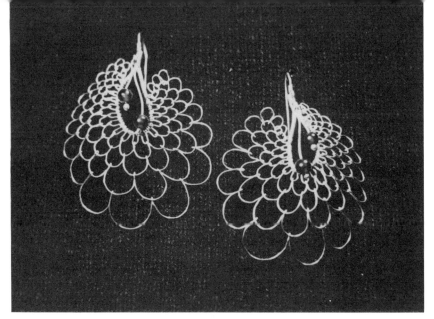

The same looping, intertwining technique was used to create this pair of earrings. Courtesy: Mary Lee Hu.

Nearly anything that can be executed in string or fiber may be translated in some form to wire. Neckpiece #1 (1966, 8" diameter) utilizes macramé stitches in fine silver. Courtesy: Mary Lee Hu.

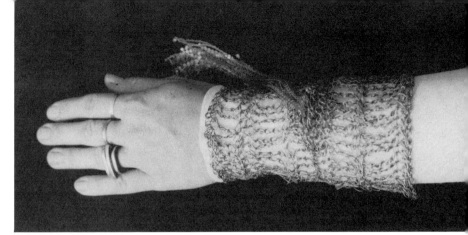

A crocheted armlet in fine silver by Nancy Cohen.
Courtesy: Nancy Cohen.

The neckpiece may be closed with wire elements
through jump rings. Courtesy: Nancy Cohen.

Bodypiece of fine and sterling silver
wire crocheted by Nancy Cohen.
Courtesy: Nancy Cohen.

Crocheted pectoral with hair, fine
and sterling silver wires. Courtesy:
Nancy Cohen.

Horse Rein

Childhood crafts like making horse rein take on new dimensions when executed in wire. Fine wires may be wrapped, pulled, and overlaid with the aid of a wooden cylinder studded with nails. The number of nails set around the top edge of the cylinder will determine the fineness of the resultant horse-rein mesh.

Wire horse rein may be made with extremely fine and flexible wires. A high-gauge precoated copper was used here. To make the horse rein, drive nails into one end of a wooden cylinder. An old wire spool works well. The number of nails determines the fineness and complexity of the product. Several inches of wire are first inserted through the cylinder and then wrapped once clockwise around each nail —moving counterclockwise around the cylinder. When all the nails have been wrapped, the wire is then wrapped around the outside of each nail, in succession. Using a crochet needle or other fine tool, the wire below is pulled out and over the top of the nail toward the inside. This process is repeated until the rein reaches the desired length. The completed form emerges through the bottom of the spool.

Fine horse rein takes a great deal of time to make, but the results are exciting. This necklace is by Nancy Cohen.

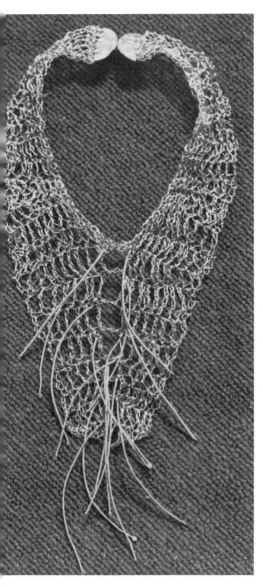

A wire necklace by Nancy Cohen employs macramé techniques.

Necklace with pendant, knitted of sterling thread, by Rolf Grude of Norway.

Weaving

Weaving of wires may be treated much as is the weaving of fibers, but traditional arrangement of warp and weft may be varied in several ways. Because of wire's unique stiffness, the final "cloth" may be shaped and twisted—or even forged and reshaped. Three-dimensional objects may also be woven since wire retains its given shape so well.

Again, Mary Lee Hu achieves exciting results by wrapping strands together, bending them away from the central axis and weaving fine wires between them. She often creates animallike constructions in this manner. And she utilizes the same techniques in creating jewelry.

Wires may be woven in as many ways as fibrous materials. Here Mary Lee Hu begins by wrapping wires along a central axis. The axial wires are sterling silver, and precoated copper wire is woven around them.

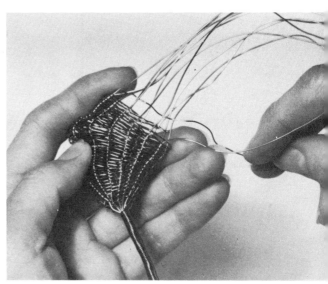

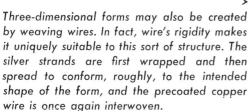

Three-dimensional forms may also be created by weaving wires. In fact, wire's rigidity makes it uniquely suitable to this sort of structure. The silver strands are first wrapped and then spread to conform, roughly, to the intended shape of the form, and the precoated copper wire is once again interwoven.

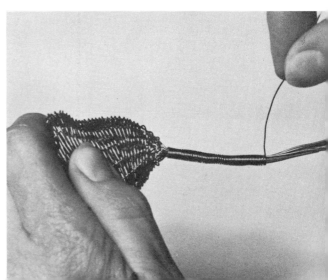

The form may be finished by wrapping the end entirely, cutting it off, or combining it with some other structure.

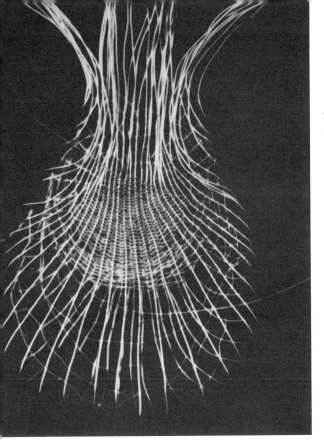

The beginnings of Neckpiece #8 show the weaving process. Courtesy: Mary Lee Hu.

Neckpiece #8 by Mary Lee Hu. A basket-woven form of silver wire. Courtesy: Mary Lee Hu.

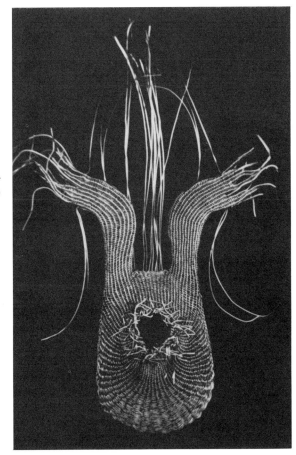

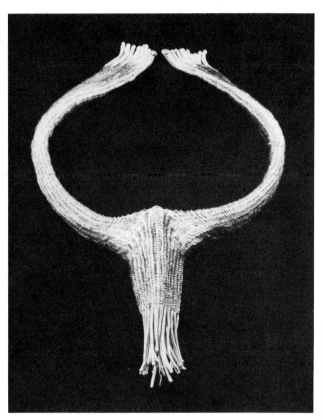

This neckpiece, woven of fine silver wire, is finished by wrapping the wire ends with more wire. The balls at the ends of the tentacles are created by gently heating the silver until it balls up. Courtesy: Mary Lee Hu.

In Neckpiece #7 (1971, 12" x 24") Mary Lee Hu used the different colors of fine and sterling silver, fine gold, and precoated copper to achieve the patterned weave. Courtesy: Mary Lee Hu.

Chapter 3

JOINING WIRE

There are two principal considerations in attaching wire: function and form.

Wire can be joined in many ways. Some techniques, such as twisting, intertwining, and linking, are purely mechanical, made possible by wire's inherent characteristics. Other ways of joining are external to the material: soldering, gluing. In choosing attachment techniques, the craftsman must consider both function and form—his purpose, the technical limitations of his material, and how technique relates to design. Where great strength is necessary because the object will be put under stress, soldering may be best. But fine wire may be obscured by solder; twisting and intertwining may provide support and integrate with a delicate form as well. Strength and stress require our attention.

Excessive strength may not be detrimental to a particular design, but time and energy have probably been wasted. When using wire as an armature for papier-mâché sculpture, for example, strong soldered joints would be superfluous, a needless expenditure of energy. Paper wrapped around the armature will provide the essential structural support; a twisted and stapled skeleton should suit the function. If a twist will do just as well as a more involved technique, do not automatically opt for the latter. Make the joint fit the job. Choose the attachment technique that offers strength *appropriate* to your purpose.

Many times, almost any kind of joint will do. There, aesthetic considerations should predominate. Just as each attachment device has a characteristic degree of strength and workability, each technique imparts a different appearance to the final product. Slick "professional-looking" projects may lead the craftsman to use solder, regardless of other considerations, since the judicious and skillful use of solder will yield fine, nearly invisible connections. Alternatively, Alexander Calder (who could have soldered his curious circus characters and human caricatures) employed only mechanical techniques. His bulky twists and loops are aesthetically as well as technically appropriate for that work; those joints complement the spontaneous, loose, comical ruse of each piece. Mary Lee Hu, who works in silver, gold, and brass wire of the finest gauges, exploits the rich *textures* achievable by combining several mechanical joining techniques in an individual piece. Her necklaces typically incorporate wire that is wrapped, interwoven, twisted, crocheted—almost never using solder. An imaginative repertoire of applications and combinations of attachment techniques charges her pieces with singular rhythm and style.

WRAPPING

One of the most elementary attachment techniques is wrapping. Wrapping can be used to reinforce a structure or to add extra dimension. It offers a very uniform texture when tightly wound around a heavier gauge wire armature. And different effects can be achieved by varying the tightness of the wrapping, the gauge of the wire, and the wire(s) being wrapped. Extra variability comes through the twisting of wires prior to wrapping. Wires which have already been twisted into double or triple strands provide the wrapping with other textures.

Mary Lee Hu wraps in many ways. The praying mantis is begun by wrapping a single strand of fine silver or sterling silver wire with another strand of the same gauge. That wrapped wire is in turn used to wrap a bundle of silver wires. Wires from that bundle are bent out at different points to become limbs and antennae of her insect. Using fine silver as the wrapping wire, she scales a dragon by strapping a length of wire loops onto its back.

Mary Lee Hu uses the wrapping technique continually, integrating the method with the design to produce a consistent and exciting texture. It is the texture, and not the attachment technique itself, that stands out.

But wrapping may be made obvious and still look good. In jewelry made of bent horseshoe nails, wire is blatantly wrapped around the nails, much as one might use rope to lash sticks together. There too, the lashed wire attachment is both functionally and aesthetically central to the design.

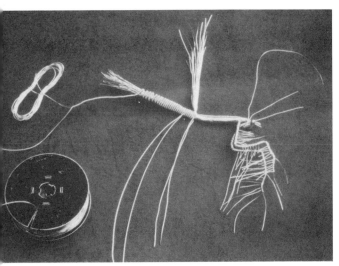

Wrapping is the simplest method of attaching wires together, but the results achieved by using it need not be unsophisticated. Mary Lee Hu's Praying Mantis began by wrapping a long strand of sterling silver wire with fine silver wire. That strand was then used to wrap many pieces of wire which serve as the body. Each piece, in turn, is bent away to form the limbs and tentacles. Some are wrapped and others remain untouched. This series courtesy: Mary Lee Hu.

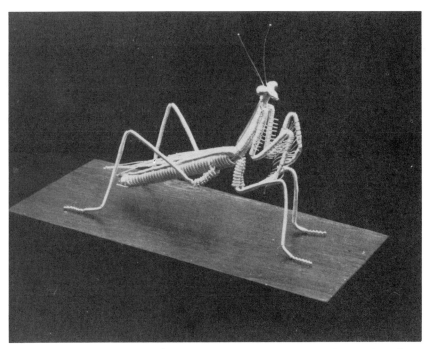

Praying Mantis (1974, 4 1/2″ long), by Mary Lee Hu, of fine and sterling silver wires.

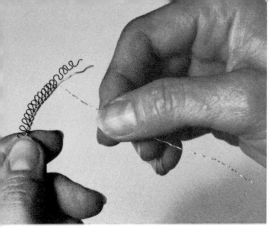

Wrapping need not be without frills. A looped strand of copper is bound to an armature of sterling with fine silver wire. Wires must always be chosen for their qualities in a given application. Here, the stiffer sterling lends support, while the soft fine silver wire wraps easily.

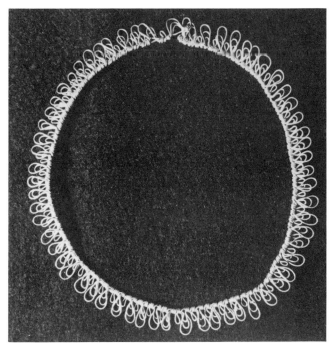

Mary Lee Hu constructed this necklace by binding three individually looped strands of silver together.

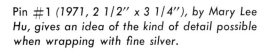

A construction very like the necklace above, except using only one set of loops in this case, was twisted into a spiral to create these earrings.

Pin #1 (1971, 2 1/2" x 3 1/4"), by Mary Lee Hu, gives an idea of the kind of detail possible when wrapping with fine silver.

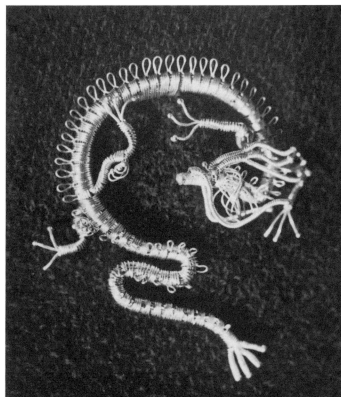

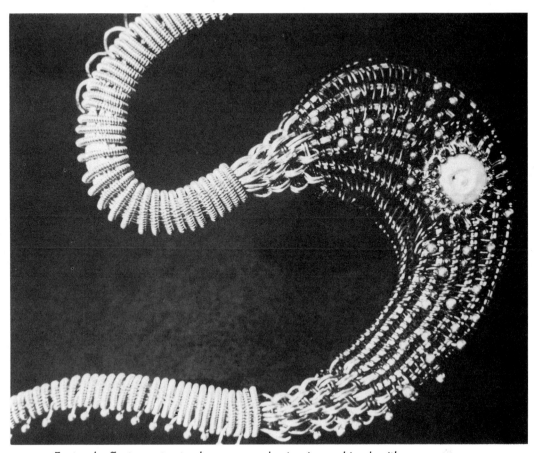

Textural effects contrast when wrapped wire is combined with woven strands.

Rudy Dorval uses wrapped, twisted, and coiled wires to create realistic figures. He combines his forms in settings to communicate stories and adventures and just to have some fun. Telephone wires with variegated insulation color the scenes.

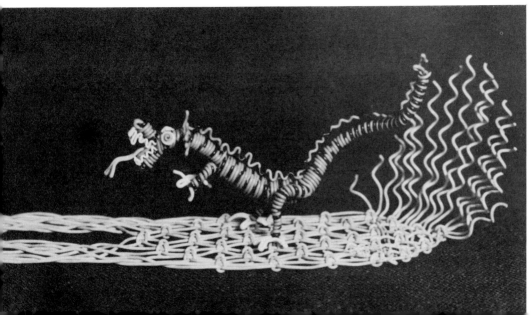

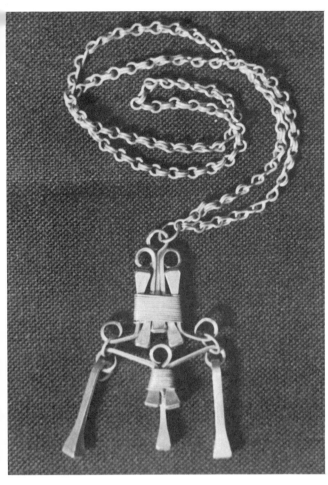

Uncomplicated wrappings lash these horseshoe nails to create a pendant.

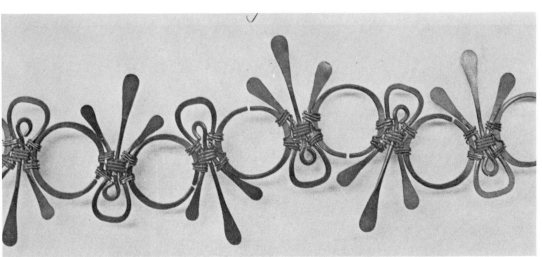

Individual units were forged and bound with soft, insulated wire.

Wrapping becomes an extremely strong structural element when used to support a wire framework. This French salad basket uses no attachment other than wrapping with fine binding wire at every joint—even the handle is of wrapped wire.

Earrings of fine, fringed silver illustrate another aspect of wrapping. Courtesy: Mary Lee Hu.

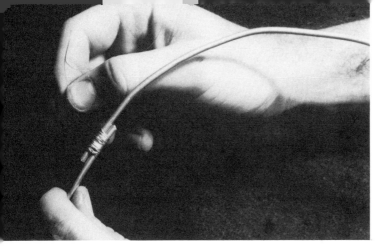

Fine binding wire is used to lash heavy aluminum wire.

White liquid glue helps keep the wire in place.

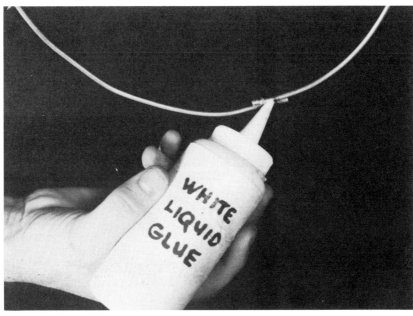

Heavy wires may also be notched slightly so that a crosspiece or binding wire will sit securely in the groove.

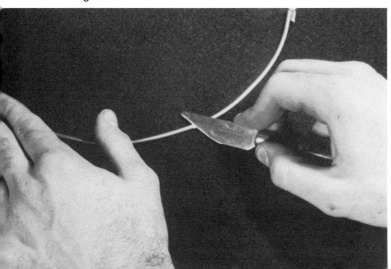

TWISTING

Wire may be attached in many ways by hand or with only a pliers: a twist is all it takes. The type of twist employed will often depend upon working conditions. In hard-to-reach places, a simple twist of two or three turns around another piece of wire will have to suffice. But as a part of the wireworker's repertoire, consider—and invent—new twists.

The twist—as basic to our use of wire as bending—opens up to the craftsman a simple but dramatic sculptural possibility. With pliers, a wire cutter, and almost any wire, spontaneously bent and twisted metal sculptures can emerge. The twist may yield gross, sweeping forms or sensitive detail. For Calder, a twist could mean a cow's udder, John D. Rockefeller's moustache, or the waist of a muscle man.

Of course, twisting as a technique, will often be combined with other methods of working wire. Wire may be mechanically inserted into other wire, especially in conjunction with the process of flattening wire (see Chapter 2). By drilling holes in the pounded piece, wire can be inserted and then hung and twisted into place.

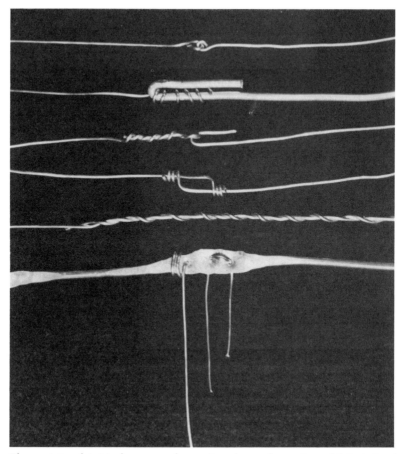

The variety of twisted, wrapped, punctured, overlapped, and intertwined attachment devices is endless.

Alexander Calder employs twisted and other mechanical joints masterfully in Rockefeller. Courtesy: Art Institute of Chicago.

Cow (1929, 6 1/2" x 16"), by Alexander Calder. Courtesy: The Museum of Modern Art.

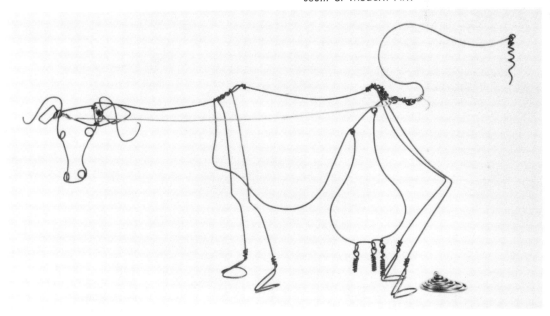

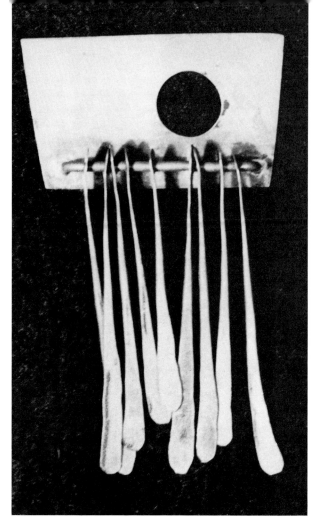

Holes were drilled in forged wire elements to attach them to the cut metal base.

John Snidecor passes fine gold wires through holes in a cast crosspiece. He flattens the ends slightly and they are held forever in place.

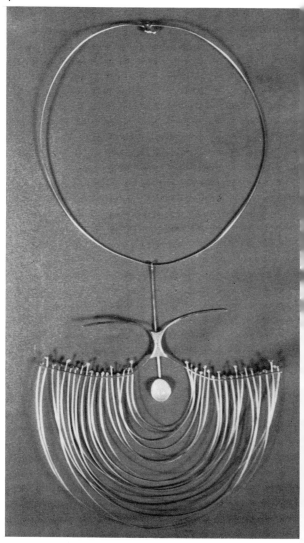

INTERTWINING

The colander is one example of wire at work. Intertwined lengths of wire hold their shape with flexibility and efficiency. A cyclone fence, for example, is simply heavy gauge wire bent in such a way that it may be intertwined and stretched between posts. The concept can readily be applied to craft. Mary Lee Hu uses intertwining in her necklaces to give a sense of rhythm and to provide a scaly look. An armature form can be "filled in" quite readily with a combination of twisting and intertwining.

Coils of wire were intertwined to create this flexible salad basket.

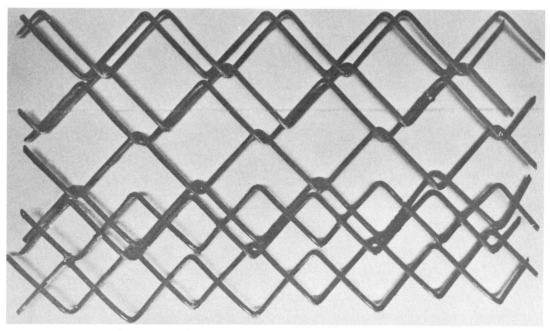

*Herbert Feuerlicht modified a section of wire cyclone fence for Interruption©.
Courtesy: Herbert A. Feuerlicht.*

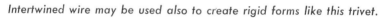

Intertwined wire may be used also to create rigid forms like this trivet.

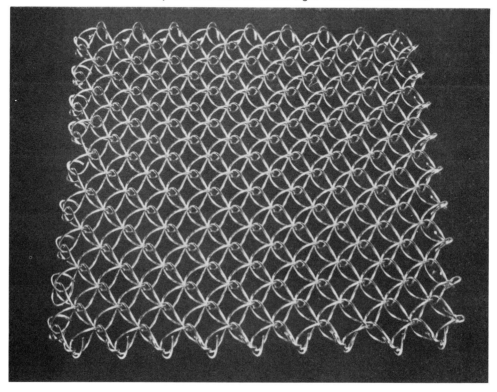

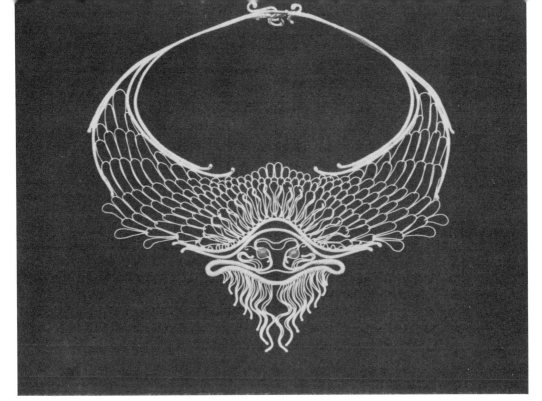

Mary Lee Hu uses many attachment techniques in combination, and she almost never uses solders and glues. In these neckpieces wires were interwoven, wrapped, and interlooped. Courtesy: Mary Lee Hu.

CAGING

One variation on wrapping, twisting, and intertwining is the caging of tumbled stones and shells. In one adaptation of wrapping technique, 14-gauge round wire is used to form a spiral cage. It is thin enough to be easily bent and wrapped, and not so thick as to detract from the contents of the cage. Using the tip of a round-nosed pliers, form a loop at the end of a length of wire. With this loop as the starting point for the spiral cage, begin coiling the wire at the base of the stone. When the coiling has reached the other end, use the pliers to form a loop which will be used for hanging the cage from a chain as a pendant. Cut off excess wire past the loop. Be certain the stone is tightly entrapped by the spiral cage. Depending on the type of wire used, it may be necessary to anneal the wire, to soften it, before caging (see Chapter 2). After annealing, clean the wire with steel wool and a soft cloth with rouge.

In making the cage, do not cover up too much of the stone; use just enough wire to cage it securely. And choose the lightest gauge wire possible to offer secure support. A 14- to 18-gauge wire should be quite sufficient.

More exotic, irregularly shaped stones may be better suited by an irregular caging technique employing twisting and intertwining. Look at the stone and its irregularities and try to determine where the wire must be wrapped to anchor the stone securely. Use a finer (20-gauge) wire for irregular caging. Begin by wrapping the wire tightly across the surfaces. Avoid regularity, try to follow contours in the stone. Where the wire intersects itself, intertwine briefly. To make certain the entire cage is tight, use the tip of a round-nosed pliers to put small crimps in the wire. This adds to the irregular touch while at the same time securing the stone. Continue this interweaving and twisting over the contours until the stone has been effectively accentuated and secured. Findings for earrings or pendant can be attached anywhere on this cage.

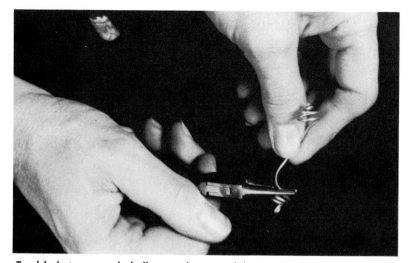

Tumbled stones and shells may be caged by wrapping them with wire. This spiral cage is formed by coiling from both ends using a round-nosed pliers.

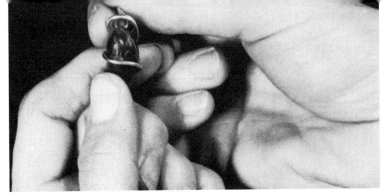

The stone is inserted into the middle of the cage, which is then twisted tight. Heavier gauge wires are appropriate for heavier stones.

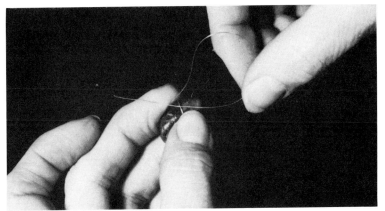

Irregular pieces may be caged by wrapping them with fine wire. Pass the wire around, through itself . . .

. . . around itself . . .

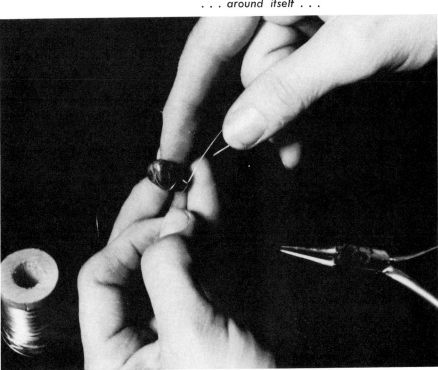

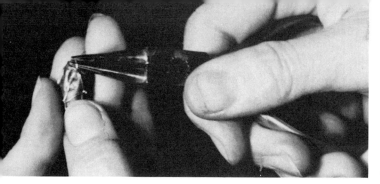

. . . and tighten the cage by twisting the wire into little kinks.

Design the cage to suit the form. A spiral cage on a conical shell makes a handsomely accented pendant.

LINKING

A classic form of wire attachment involves the link. Rings made of wire have been used extensively over centuries. Suits of jade armor worn by Chinese warriors were linked with wire rings. Hill tribe necklaces from Northern Thailand use links to connect decorative metal plates. And of course jump rings of all shapes, metals, and designs are combined into decorative chains—a staple of the jewelry business.

A variety of commercially manufactured jump rings are available. They are generally sold by the gross and are relatively inexpensive. But links are easily made with wire, a dowel stick, and a saw or wire snips.

Choose a round form of the same diameter as the rings desired. Anything will do—from a knitting needle to a wooden dowel, to a piece of pipe. If you use a square or irregular shape, your links will assume that shape. Begin by making links with 16- or 18-gauge wire. Holding the dowel firmly in hand, or, better yet, locking it in a bench vise, wrap the wire tightly around the form. Each revolution becomes one link. Wind the wire evenly until you have a long coil which has no gaps between rings.

There are several ways of cutting the coil into jump rings. One is to leave the coil on the dowel and, using a fine jeweler's saw, cut through each link one at a time. To get the best results, cut slowly. Links generally function best when there are no gaps caused by inaccurate cutting.

An alternative method is to remove the coil from the rod, pass the jeweler's saw blade through the center of the coil, and again, cut the links. A third, simpler, faster, but coarser method is to slide the coil off and snip each individual link with wire snips. This last method may leave small nibs and unevenness when the ends of the rings are matched. This can be remedied with the use of a small file.

With this simple technique, and with the variety of wire and dowels available, the potential for combining links into different chains is limitless. Jump rings can be pounded flat to achieve different shapes and textures. Rings can be made with square or half-round wire. Add another dimension to the process by varying the rhythm of combined links. Try double ring chains, or alternate single and double, double and triple, one long and one short.

A chain can be interspaced with beads on short lengths of wire. Loops made with a round-nosed pliers at the ends of wire lengths serve as ready connectors to other links.

Remember, however, that a chain is only as strong as its weakest link. If a chain is to be put under *any* stress it will be necessary to solder each link (as discussed below) into an indivisible ring as you proceed in the link-ing process. For loose hanging chains, however, soldering may be optional.

Links are most easily made from uniform coils of wire. Silver wire has been wrapped around a wooden dowel; when the wire has been sawed through, individual links will fall away.

Using pliers, interlocking rings may be com-bined into a plethora of chain designs.

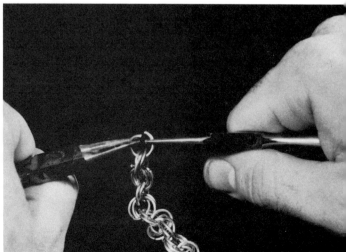

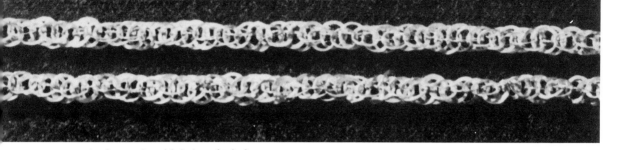

A chain of gold links which have been pounded flat and linked in opposition takes on a cylindrical shape.

A few of thousands of chain designs (from the top): (1) three links soldered at a single point are joined, each center link passing through the three above, (2) a single link chain in which the sides of each link have been slightly flattened, (3) a more complex design involving flat wire passing through round wire links.

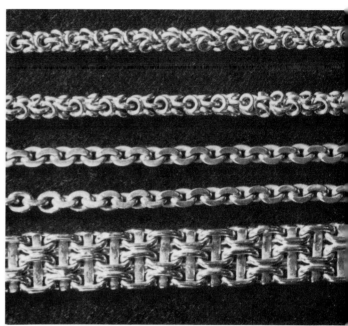

Every single sterling silver wire link in this chain mail necklace was soldered by Peder Musse of Denmark. The links were gradually reduced in size so that the piece lies flat around the neck.

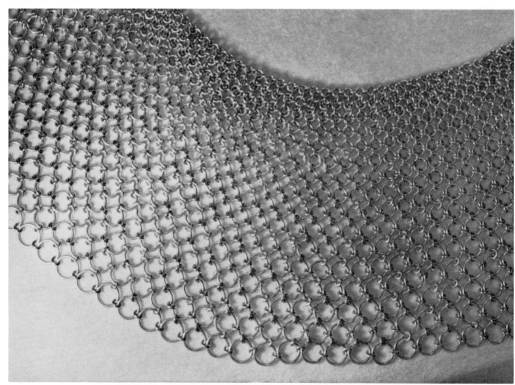

The Yao hill tribe of northern Thailand uses links to connect decorated plates
to form a traditional woman's necklace. Fine wire springs connect the bangles.

Because horseshoe nails are soft and malleable they can be readily linked together with only a pliers and hammer.

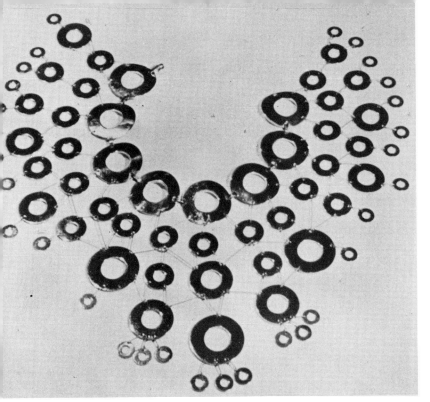

Here Mary Ann Scherr has strung stainless steel washers with tempered stainless steel wire. Courtesy: Mary Ann Scherr.

Links attach all the wires used in this necklace by Mary Ann Scherr. Courtesy: Mary Ann Scherr.

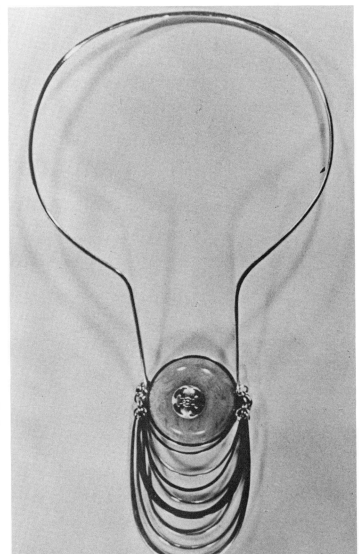

ADHESIVE ATTACHMENTS: COLD SOLDER, EPOXY, AND MIRACLE GLUES

Cold solder is essentially a glue for metals. The cold solders (so called because they are applied without heat) are glues mixed with powdered metal. They produce a metallic look when hard and are good for many attachment jobs. Cold solders, however, like all adhesives used with metals, are not recommended where great strength is required.

Two-part epoxies have many applications with wire—especially for creating seasonal ornaments, embedments, light wire pieces. Krazy Glue[R], an all-purpose miracle adhesive, can be used for unstressed wire attachment as well. Always clean metal surfaces before applying the adhesives.

Although adhesives represent an easy and familiar mode of attachment for most of us, they are not a primary technique, but rather a supplemental one, in wirework.

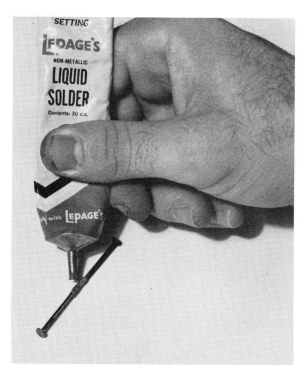

Cold solder is an adhesive that looks like metal when hard.

Cold solder or epoxy cement works well for attachments that will not be put under much stress.

Quick-drying two-part epoxy is mixed thoroughly and applied to the nail designs.

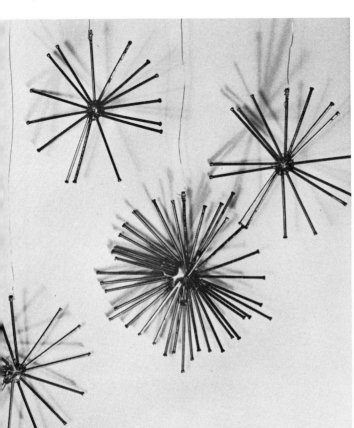

Metal snowflakes?

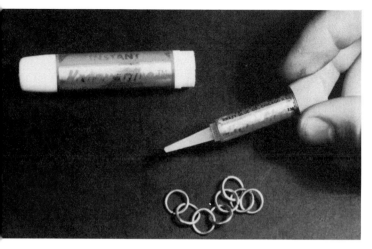

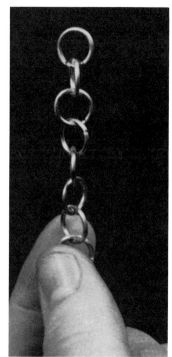

Miracle adhesives, like Krazy Glue^R, will attach just about anything (sometimes including fingers, so watch out).

Krazy Glue^R creates a good bond in only five seconds, but it will not withstand much stress.

Gini Merrill constructed this miniature bicycle with fine wires and Krazy Glue^R.

SOLDERING

The word solder derives from the Latin *solidare,* to make solid, and that is, essentially, what this attachment technique does.

Soldered connections remain secure even when subjected to physical stress—torsional strain, expansion and contraction of the metals due to temperature variation, corrosion. And soldering is an important means of augmenting the strength of other attachment devices such as links and cages. The soldering techniques are simple and effective. With a minimum of tools, metals can be connected so well, at times, that the point of attachment will prove stronger than the wire itself.

Solders generally divide into two categories: soft solder (made of lead and tin with a low melting point of 400° to 700° F.) and hard solder (also called silver solder, made of various combinations of silver, copper, and zinc, melting in the range of 800° to about 1500° F.). These solders can be used to connect most metals by melting the solder into joints. Placed on a joint, the solder alloy melts, and then flows by capillary action into cracks less than 4/1000th of an inch wide to effect a bond. Solders actually mix with the parent metal to form a new alloyed metal bond.

The materials and tools for soldering are simple and inexpensive. And the technique's versatility and utility with regard to wire art make it an indispensable addition to the wireworker's repertoire.

Five essential steps are involved in the soldering process:

1) All metal surfaces, including the solder itself, must be perfectly clean.
2) The metal to be joined must be fitted together tightly at the joint.
3) Flux, a chemical essential to effective soldering, is applied.
4) The solder is placed in position spanning the joint.
5) Heat is applied.

This is the basic process, but each step will be considered in somewhat more detail; a failure in any one of the five steps will lead to a failure in soldering. Once these simple procedures are mastered and routinized, the craftsman can produce perfect bonds time and again.

Hard Soldering

Known also as silver solder (because of its high silver content), hard solder can be used generally with silver, brass, copper, and many other metals, with the noted exception of aluminum. Composed of varying percentages of silver, copper, and zinc along with some traces of other elements, silver solder for the craftsman's purpose is generally available in three grades: easy (melts around 1320°F), medium (around 1390°F), and hard (around 1420°F). Available in sheets (of various gauges), strips, pellets, files, rods, powders, hard solders can also be bought in different tones which will match the color of the work. The different forms of solder allow hard soldering to be done in a number of ways: using stick solder and a paste flux, or using small chips (snippets) of solder and flux, for example. The form of solder and method of soldering should be dictated by convenience in the working situation.

Grades of Solder

As mentioned above, hard solder is available in three grades—easy, medium, and hard—signifying the temperatures necessary to make each melt and flow. In theory, when many soldered joints must be made on a single piece, different grades of solder should be used. Hard, which melts at the highest temperature would be applied first, medium next, and easy last. The reason is that if the same temperature solder were used for each joint, all previous joints would run the risk of melting again. In practice, however, it may be more efficacious to use only easy solder or only easy and medium grades. On most pieces it will often be possible to control the heating of the form so that other joints will be saved. Consider this, then, in light of the requirements of each piece—but remember that for delicate work the high degree of heat required by hard solder may be injurious to the metal.

Preparing the Solder

If using three grades of silver solder (4 mm thickness will generally work well), mark the solders with letters signifying which is which—to the eye the solder will look alike unless marked for identification.

Clean the surfaces of the solder using emery cloth or steel wool. All gross dirt and grease must be removed if the solder is to function effectively. After cleaning, handle the solder through paper to avoid new grease deposits. With lightweight snips or scissors, cut the solder into small (1/32″) square chips. These snippets will be applicable in all soldering operations. Again, keep the easy, medium, and hard solders separate, and when choosing a solder for a specific job, follow a simple rule: use the solder having the lowest melting and flowing temperature that will still perform the job effectively. Excess heat increases the possibility of damaging the metal.

Preparing Wire to Be Soldered

Every metal surface that will be part of the joint area must be thoroughly cleaned before soldering—and that means totally free of not only shellacs and paint, but grease, dirt, and the film that exists on all metals called "oxides." If there is any oxidation on the metal to be joined, the solder will not flow onto that surface; it will just ball up. Clean first with emery cloth, a wire brush, scraper, steel wool or file. Cleaning can also be done chemically by means of "pickling" (see below).

After cleaning, the pieces of wire to be joined must be butted so that they fit together as closely as possible. Solder cannot bridge large gaps. If necessary, binding wire (20-gauge soft iron wire is good) can be used to brace the pieces together. Also, a variety of soldering jigs can be purchased or improvised. It is worth repeating that however you choose to butt the pieces to be soldered, the juncture must be small—around a few thousandths of an inch. The pieces of parent metal should appear to touch.

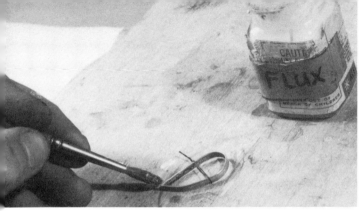

Before soldering, all surfaces must be cleaned thoroughly and the joint must be butted as tightly as possible. Here, iron binding wire was used to hold the ends of a teardrop of flat wire together. Flux is applied to the joint by brush.

Flux

As already mentioned, most metal is covered with a thin, nonmetallic layer called an oxide. Scrubbing with emery cloth will not remove oxides—the removal must be done by chemical means. The oxide forms an insulating barrier between metals. As long as it exists, no two metals can make actual physical contact. If contact cannot be made, then the intermetallic solvent process of soldering cannot proceed. Readily available chemicals called "fluxes" must be applied to all metal surfaces at a joint before soldering. A flux removes the nonmetallic oxide film and keeps that film from re-forming during heating (heat generates new oxide buildup).

Fluxes, when heated, turn glasslike, and are therefore helpful as indicators of the approach of the solder's melting temperature. Before the necessary melting temperature is reached, the flux will harden into a glassy coating. At that point, the flux becomes pasty and sticky and the solder that has moved during the initial heating may be prodded back into place and held by the now sticky flux.

The fluxes used in hard soldering are prepared in paste, solid, and liquid forms. Borax, which comes in powder, sticks, or compressed cones, can be mixed with a little water to make an inexpensive flux. But many perfectly good commercial all-purpose fluxes can also be used effectively. If the surfaces are not well covered, more flux can be added during the preliminary stages of heating the form.

To coat the solder with flux, dip the solder into the paste or liquid, using tweezers. If the flux, when applied to the metal or solder, rolls off, then try cleaning the surfaces again mechanically—they have to be greaseless.

Placement of Solder

Use a brush dipped in flux to pick up bits of solder and transfer them to the joints.

If you are using snippets of solder, then the snippet should touch both parts that are to be attached. Avoid using too much solder—the less, the stronger the bond and the less the unsightly excess. Especially in working with wire, an excess of solder (unless intended as a special effect) detracts from the fine cylindrical shape of the medium by distorting it.

In the placement of solder, technical considerations enter into the decision. If the job will require one soldered joint in fairly close proximity to another, consider the use of hard, medium, and easy grades of solder. Another way of controlling the heat in the presence of many solder joints is through the application of yellow ochre or other agents discussed below.

Precut snippets of medium grade hard solder (1/32" square) may be picked up with a brush slightly wet with flux . . .

. . . and placed on the joint so that it bridges the joint in the wire.

Soldering should be performed on only certain materials: asbestos block or board, magnesium soldering block, charcoal block, or any other flameproof material recommended for soldering work. The magnesium soldering block, which is made of carbonate of magnesium combined with asbestos, will last longer than the charcoal block and will allow the insertion of steel pins to position works to be soldered. The charcoal block—a favorite of many craftsmen—provides a good surface that will not burn and that retains and reflects the applied heat. Wrap the new charcoal block in a grid of binding wire to keep it from falling apart too fast.

Methods of Heating

The primary means of heating metal for soldering which we will consider here is with the propane torch. (A discussion of the use of the soldering iron follows.) Small, inexpensive hand-held torches that come with different nozzles and replaceable bottles of gas are best for the craftsman's uses (unless he has access to professional oxyacetylene or acetylene equipment). A Bernz-O-Matic[R] propane torch with medium nozzle will work quite well in most applications, although for fine jewelry work finer flames are necessary.

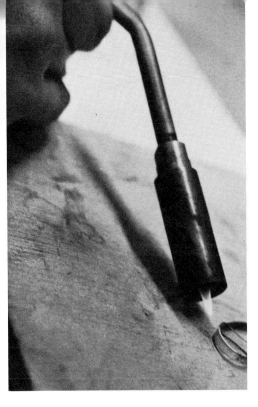

The heating operation may be performed on a sheet of asbestos (as here), on charcoal, or on wire mesh. The flame from the propane torch is played over the wire evenly—never focusing on the joint or the solder. Solder flows toward heat, and when the metal is hot enough the solder will melt and flow into the joint. If the piece is not heated evenly, however, the solder may not flow onto both sides. Flux and oxidation can be removed by dropping the piece into a pickle, but always remove the binding wire first or unsightly flashes will be left on the metal where the acid contacts the iron.

This wire design was created by interweaving pieces of brass piano wire and soldering them into place.

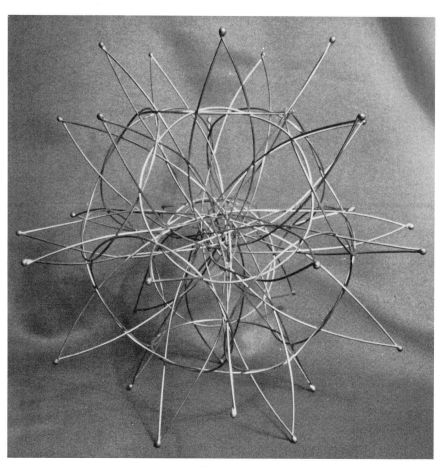

Interwoven, soldered brass wire designs.

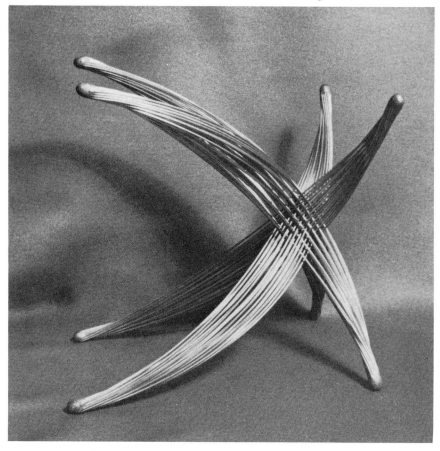

This Mexican belt buckle is made by soldering square silver wire to the silver base.

A necklace of brass wire soldered onto brass and silver sheet, by Maurice Abramson.

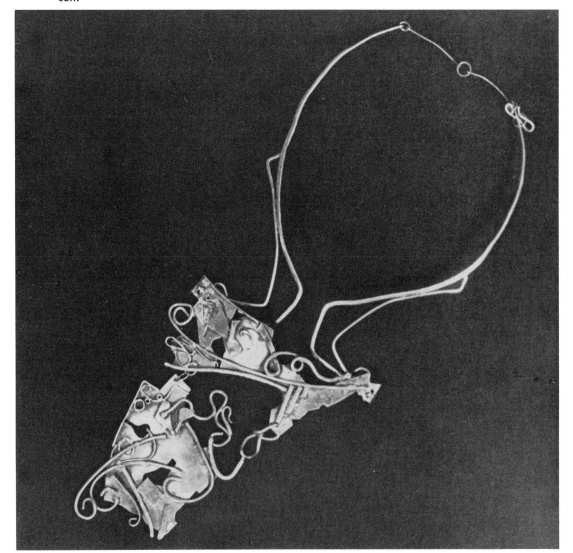

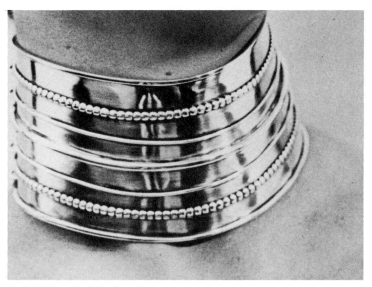

Using solder, Mary Ann Scherr appliquéd square and round and beaded wires to a silver choker. Courtesy: Mary Ann Scherr.

The torch is easier to use than a soldering iron since the heat can be readily regulated and the flame heats the wire faster and covers a larger area of metal.

To light a torch, use a friction spark lighter, match, or alcohol lamp. Open the valve on the gas bottle just enough to light a small flame. Then the torch can be adjusted as high as needed. When starting a torch, always point the nozzle away from you.

The size of the flame is controlled by feeding more or less gas through the valve. For soldering small pieces—and in most wirework—a small pointed flame will serve best, although for other processes, such as annealing, a softer, larger flame will be preferred.

After the object has been fluxed and solder has been properly cleaned and placed on the fitted joint, heat the metal by playing the flame over the wire. The hottest part of the flame will be the part between the outside tip of the flame and the tip of the inner, different-colored, cone of the flame. Play the flame over the whole metal area, and avoid heating any one area more than another. Avoid burning the flux with direct flame contact. Do not apply direct heat to the solder when working with a torch. Keep the torch moving in a rotating manner, bringing the entire wire area up to temperature evenly. Never train the flame on one spot for any length of time. After the joint turns a dull red, or else when the flux begins to fuse, concentrate the flame closer to the joint and the solder. Otherwise the heat will dissipate and it will take longer to reach the flow temperature of the solder. When flow temperature is reached, the bead of solder should enter the joint by capillary action. Remove the heat source from the wire immediately as the solder begins to flow.

It is usually advisable to do soldering in a semidark room—out of direct light—because the flow of the solder can best be anticipated and regulated by studying the changing color of the parent metal. If, for example, the soldering has not flowed into the joint by the time the metal has become bright red, something in the process was done improperly—

Peacock Chimes (36" x 15" x 6"), by William Bowie, is made of copper, steel, and bronze. The coarse soldered connections are intended to be completely visible; they are part of the rough-and-ready effect. Courtesy: William Bowie.

Tightrope Balancing Act (10 1/2" high), by Earl Krentzin, illustrates wire's potential. Everything, from the toppling towers and wire net to twisted hoops and tiny chairs, was constructed of wire. Courtesy: Kennedy Galleries.

the cleaning, fitting, fluxing, or heating. Stop and begin again before excessive heat damages the metal.

Do not be alarmed. But begin anew and prepare the metal and solder, taking care to clean away any oxide or dirt that has developed.

Occasionally during the initial heating process the contraction of solder and metal will cause the solder to "jump" away from its original position. As the flux heats, however, it becomes more tacky and, by using a stainless-steel skewer to prod the solder into place again, proper positioning will be achieved.

It is essential to reach the flow temperature of the solder *quickly*. Flux does not have great endurance under prolonged or extreme heat, and if the action of the flux or the solder fails, then oxides will form on the metal, frustrating any continuing soldering efforts.

Controlling Solder Flow

Solder flows toward heat. Controlling the flow is often a matter of controlling which piece—or part of a piece—heats earliest and gets hottest. Although this fact may be of little importance in the fusion of the butted ends of two wires, in soldering parallel rods it can be used to good advantage. By moving the flame, solder can be drawn in a specific direction to seal a seam.

There are a variety of solder-inhibiting pastes that stop the flow of solder to areas which should not be clogged with the alloy (such as pin backs, or places where purity of line is especially important). These inhibiting pastes are also used to prevent the unsoldering of already soldered joints. Yellow ochre (an impure iron ore also known as loam) or powdered rouge (a ferric oxide) can be mixed with a little water or gum tragacanth and painted on the metal. When soldering is completed, remove the pastes (which become hard under the heat) with a stiff brush in hot water. Remove all such inhibiting pastes before pickling, to avoid contamination of the pickling solution.

Using Stick Solder

To solder along long joints, and for many nonlevel wire applications, stick solder has advantages over the snippet. Generally available in rods 20″ long and of 20 gauge, this form of solder can be applied directly. The stick of solder is coated with flux which is allowed to dry before soldering. Bringing the temperature of the parent metal up to the flow point of the solder quickly, solder is hand-fed into (and all along) the joint.

Taking Off the Flux

To remove the flux and any oxidation after the soldering has finished, wash the piece in hot water. If the flux does not come off readily, either too little flux was applied to begin with, or the piece was heated for too long a time, or the heat was too great. Remove any excess by water soaking, emery cloth, or by pickling in heated acid solution.

Pickling

Pickling is a process that follows annealing and soldering, and effectively removes scales, oxides, and other impurities on the surface of metal. Most craftsmen dunk soldered forms directly into the pickle after soldering.

The pickle is an acid solution made up of water and dilute sulphuric acid. Add the sulphuric acid to the water, one part acid to ten parts water. WARNING: *Always* add the acid to the water, never vice versa. If water is added to the acid, the acid particles have a tendency to explode apart.

The pickle can also be made with Sparex^R, a noncorrosive powder mixed with water. It contains no acid and is nonflammable and nonexplosive and requires no special storage. If using the traditional sulphuric acid pickle, mix and contain the pickle in a Pyrex^R container with a lid on it. Before using, make the pickle solution slightly warm, using any gentle heat source.

Pickle is good for cleaning brass, copper, silver, and other metals, and is also good for bleaching metals.

Work can be put into the pickle while it is still solder-hot, provided the red color has gone out of the metal. Never drop the soldered piece in with the binding wire still on it—it will leave stains on the work. Also, never put fingers into the solution (it is acid!), and *always* use tongs made of brass, nickel, or copper (never iron or steel).

Soft Soldering

Soft solder generally flows below 700°F. It creates a weaker bond than the silver solder provides, but it is used where the strength of silver solder is not of primary importance. It can be used to attach silver, gold, brass, bronze, nickel, zinc, lead, pewter, and copper, although generally it is not applied to precious metals.

Soft solder attaches metal by virtue of an intermetallic solution which it forms with the parent metal at low temperatures. A solution among metals does not effect a physical change as occurs in silver soldering or welding; it is, instead, a chemical attachment technique.

The most common soft solder is an alloy made up of tin and lead. "Half and half" (50 percent tin and 50 percent lead) is the most commonly marketed form of soft solder. There are solders that melt at different temperatures, depending on the amount of tin in the alloy. The more tin, the higher the melting point. Half and half melts and flows at 360–420°F, while pure tin (100 percent), which is used often in soldering parts to be exposed to food, melts and flows at a higher range, 450–575°F. The strongest soft solder (having the greatest stress resistance) contains 63 percent tin, but since 63 percent is not far from a 50–50 percent mix, the latter suffices.

Soft solder comes in solid bars, wires, ribbons, angular shapes, foil, powder, a paste (called fusion solder, which contains flux for one-step application), and in flux core wire. The flux-core wire solder typically comes in 1/8", 3/32", and 1/16" diameters for consumer use. Different-size cores are also available for different types and amounts of flux. The regular-size flux core is generally recommended for craft use. Sheet-form soft solder is cut into snippets and prepared for soldering in the same manner as the silver solder described earlier.

Soft Solder Fluxes

The fluxes for soft solder work on the same principles as those used in silver soldering. But the flux chemicals themselves are different from the borax or all-purpose ones used for hard soldering.

There are four basic types of fluxes for soft solder:

Chloride (also called "acid") flux, which contains different inorganic salts like zinc chloride or ammonium chloride (sal ammoniac), is effective on most metals except for aluminum and magnesium. It is the most corrosive of the soft solder fluxes. Popular soldering pastes are chloride flux put in the form of an emulsion of chloride solution and grease.

Organic base flux, although less adapted to general application than chloride flux, is less corrosive. It is considered an intermediate flux because of its reduced stability under prolonged heat exposure.

Rosin flux is a totally noncorrosive material which is effective on many metals. Only when it gets hot does rosin flux become corrosive, attaching chemically to oxides to remove them from metal, and allow soldering to occur. When it cools, rosin flux becomes inert again. Prepared soldering pastes like Nokorode[R] have the action of rosin flux.

Activated rosin flux, the fourth flux type, is also noncorrosive, but it has the advantage of being as effective as the highly active chloride flux.

Soft Soldering Process

As before, in silver soldering, clean and fit the metal meticulously. Apply flux in the same manner as in hard soldering. A smaller flame is needed in soft soldering, but, again, the soldering should be completed in as short a time as possible. If using snippets, place one on the fluxed joint, then play the flame over the metal until flow temperature is reached. The solder will ball up, then flow freely into the joint. Remove the heat source from the metal. Wipe excess solder from the joint using a pad of cloth before the excess solder solidifies. Let the piece cool, then get rid of the flux residue with pickle or hot water and soap.

If using the flux-core solder wire, still apply some flux to the joint area. Play the flame over the metal for a second or two or three. Then reapply flux. Having reached the flow temperature in the abutted metals, touch the flux-core solder wire to the joint. Let it flow, following the heat of the parent metal and *not* the heat of direct flame. If using solder rod with no flux core, dip the rod into flux before bringing it to the hot metal.

Excess solder not removed by hot wiping can be filed off with a float file (a file designed especially for use on soft metals) or with emery cloth or another abrasive material.

Aluminum Soldering

Aluminum soldering is a special case, outside the silver solder and soft solder classes. If highly heated with zinc salt, the zinc can be reduced and fused to the aluminum. This requires special aluminum solder and aluminum flux, and is only effective on high grade 2s, 3s, or 4s aluminum.

Using a Soldering Iron

The soldering iron comes with a copper tip which heats up electrically. The principle of the iron is the same as with the flame, only it is the iron, instead of the quick flame, which is used to heat the parent metal and melt the solder.

Only the lead/tin soft solder has low-enough melting point for use with the soldering irons. Other solders require the use of a flame.

Irons are available in sizes ranging from less than an ounce to two pounds. A 6- to 8-ounce tool is generally efficient for craft use. The iron needs to be large enough to hold and impart sufficient heat.

To use the iron it should first be "tinned." This process makes the solder flow more easily. The tip of the iron is cleaned, coated with flux, heated up, and then coated with a layer of solder.

Once the iron is covered and loaded with solder, hold it at the fluxed point where soldering is to begin. When enough heat has been transferred to the metal from the iron, the solder will begin to flow. Preheating of the work to a temperature just below the flow temperature of the solder will help the solder flow quickly. When using flux-core solder wire, do not just melt the flux-solder into the iron; rather, make the *side* of the iron and the heat of the metal do the melting. If you were to put solder and flux core on the iron instead of on the exact point of adhesion, the flux would not leave the iron. The solder would roll onto the joint without flux and would not flow.

MAKING A SOLDERED RING BOWL

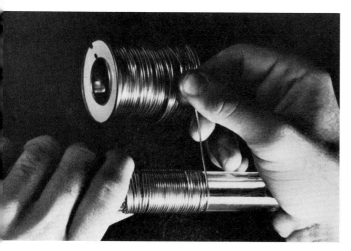

Copper wire jump rings were made by wrapping 14-gauge wire around a dowel of the desired diameter.

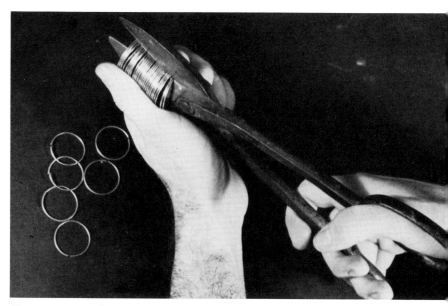

The rings were then cut, one by one, with a metal shears. Uneven ends were filed flat so that the joints would butt properly.

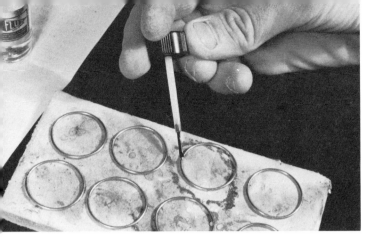

Each ring was laid flat on asbestos and painted, at the joint, with an all-purpose flux.

Bits of solder—this time cut from a rod rather than a sheet—are picked up with a fluxed brush and placed over the individual joints.

A handy gadget with alligator clips braced the rings in position so that they could be soldered to form a bowl. A propane torch was used throughout.

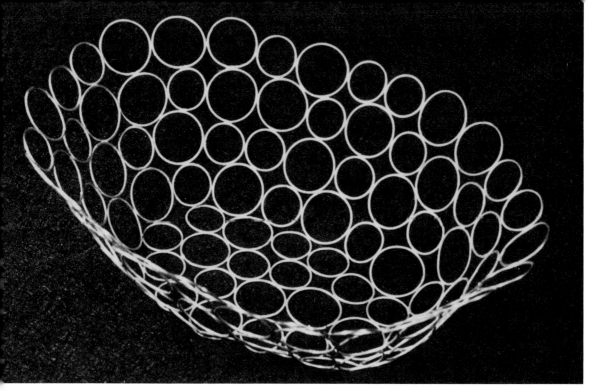

Simplicity of design rings true.

The effort bears fruit.

A CHAIN MADE OF FOLDED LINKS

Many traditional soldering techniques involve the use of a blowpipe directed through an alcohol lamp's flame. A village silversmith of northern Thailand here places silver jump rings on a homemade charcoal block. He applies a mixture of flux and solder.

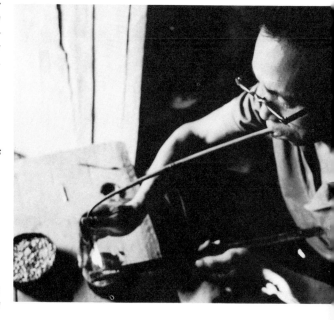

By controlling blowpipe and links he directs the flame.

One type of chain is made by squeezing each soldered link at its middle with a tweezers.

The flattened links are folded over each other to produce a chain.

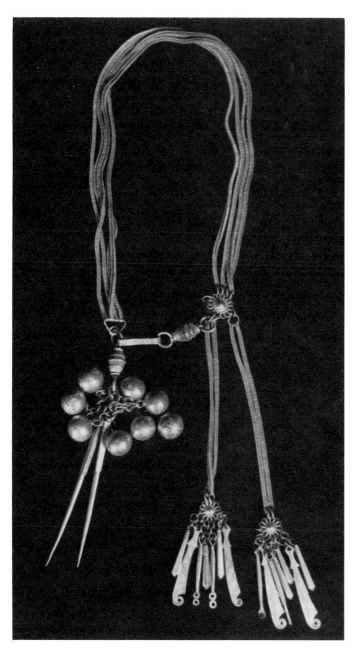

A variety of tools and decorations are attached to the chains at their ends—including ear, nose, and tooth picks. For Thai women of this tribe, silver chain is wealth: the more you wear, the richer you are.

CLIFFORD EARL'S CONSTRUCTIONS

Clifford Earl constructs fanciful ships and flying machines using wire and simple tools. Here he curls wire with needle-nosed pliers. This series courtesy: Clifford Earl.

Wheel shapes are made by wrapping wire around a metal form. Clifford Earl uses a variety of found and homemade jigs to form wire.

More jigs for bending wheels of different diameters.

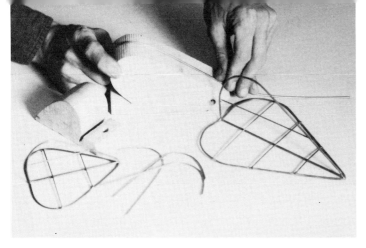

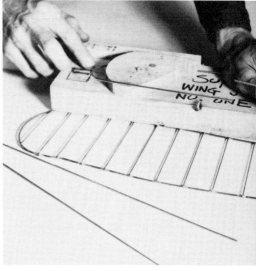

Wing jigs, like most others, may be used hundreds of times. Clifford Earl makes notations on each one describing its function and idiosyncrasies.

He attaches the wires, using an acetylene torch and stick solder.

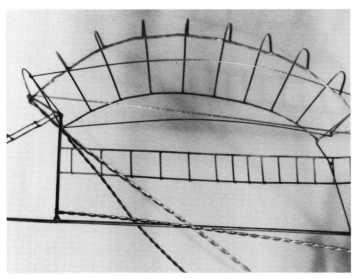

Details of the partially constructed form.

One technique for finishing the ends of wires is to heat them until a small bead forms. Beading serves the practical function of eliminating unfinished ends, and the result may be decorative as well.

Rounded wire tips are effective in the wrought-iron-like pattern on the ship's stern.

This detail shows the wooden and metal people/objects that inhabit the ship.

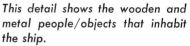

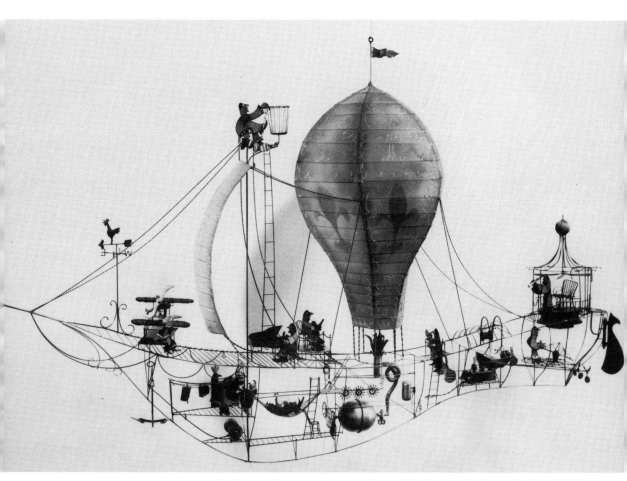

Sailing Ship #1 (1974), by Clifford Earl. This series courtesy: Clifford Earl.

Chapter 4

WIRE IN TWO DIMENSIONS

Wire's linearity lends the medium to two-dimensional applications: embedded on the top of a box; bent, pounded, and soldered into patterns resembling line drawings; formed as dams in enameling; embroidered on screening. Wire easily translates techniques employing string, yarn, and, in a sense, pen and ink into something distinctly wire. Wherever it is used, wire retains its own character in the final product.

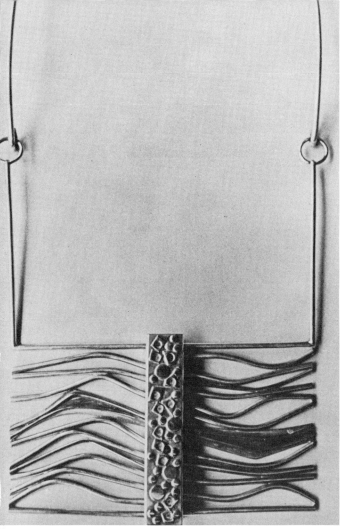

Heart Monitoring Necklace *contains a space in its center to house the electronics. The form is of gold and silver wires, with an appliqué of slices of round wire on the center post. Courtesy: Mary Ann Scherr.*

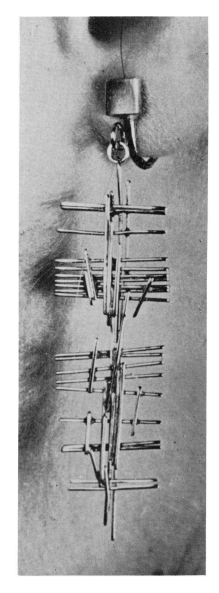

These stainless steel wire earrings by Mary Ann Scherr suggest segments of overlapping planes. Courtesy: Mary Ann Scherr.

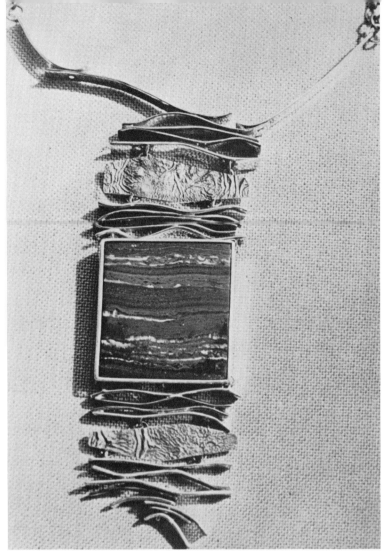

Flat and rectangular gold wire provides the perfect setting for tiger eye strata. Courtesy: Mary Ann Scherr.

Bird of Paradise III (1964), by Richard Lippold. Courtesy: Willard Gallery, collection of Nelson A. Rockefeller.

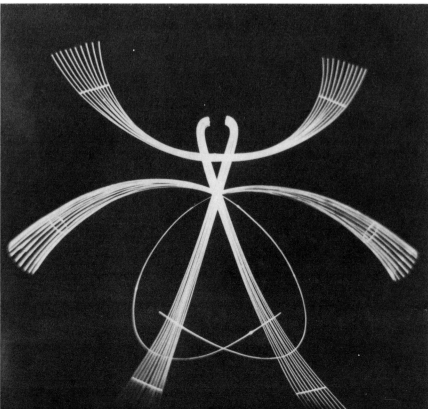

WIRE SILHOUETTES

Seven or eight hundred years ago, during the Sung dynasty of China, "iron pictures" were first created. Made by hammering red hot iron into stylized flowers, human figures, landscapes, and insects, the iron pictures were used as wall panels.

Finished pieces were coated with black paint to contrast distinctly when mounted in a frame against white paper or silk.

These pictures are still made today in China—executed with forceful strokes within the elegant classical style.

Using several different gauges of wire, a hammer, pliers, soft soldering tools, or cold solder, wire panels resembling line drawings or silhouettes can be created. Begin by sketching a design on paper. Try to develop simple uncomplicated ideas.

Bend the wire to shape with pliers. Consider the use of forged elements in the design. Since the piece will not be put under stress, adhesives such as Krazy Glue[R], epoxy, or cold solder have logical application. Soft solder may also be employed effectively.

Wire may be used to create fine silhouettes or to reproduce line drawings. This traditional craft form developed in China.

These pictures were made of forged, twisted, and soldered iron wire.

Spidery-Form©, by Herbert A. Feuerlicht, makes good use of wire's linearity. Courtesy: Herbert A. Feuerlicht.

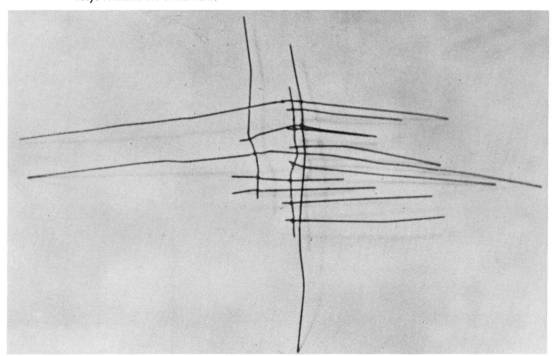

Wire as line drawing has had application throughout the world for centuries, as in this traditional window panel at a wat in Thailand.

WIRE SPIRAL JEWELRY

The flat, linked forms shown here are of ancient origin; a relic of Egyptian tombs and ancient Greece, the design survives in Indonesia and other modern cultures, too. The graceful coil can be readily adapted to myriad uses, especially in jewelry.

If working in silver or stiff metal, it will probably be necessary to anneal the wire first (see Chapter 2). Use 16-gauge round wire. One link unit of small size will require about 8 inches of wire. Experiment with scrap wire first to determine the exact length necessary to achieve swirls of the preferred size.

After annealing, use the tip of round-nosed pliers to form a ring of the smallest possible size at both ends of the wire. Hand-coil the wire from one end in a counterclockwise direction, making larger and larger concentric circles around that original loop. Complete four, five, or six entire revolutions (depending on the length of wire used), making certain the coil is tightly and uniformly wrapped. Beginning from the other end, repeat this process in a clockwise direction until about 3″ of wire remains between the coils. The coil pair should be of identical size.

Bend the wire at the exact middle of the central length using needle-nosed pliers, until the two coils meet, leaving a large loop between them. Always keep the coils flat and in the same plane.

Clean and polish the coils using emery cloth.

Then fold the long loop into a hook at the back of the coils using pliers as shown. The hook should be parallel to the plane of the coils.

That completes a single unit. Repeat this process for as many units as necessary. To assemble the links, slip each one through the loop of the next—they should overlap slightly and thereby hide the hook at back. Once all the units are interlinked, turn the chain over and tap it gently with a rubber mallet. This will set the hooks at a uniform level. For a high gloss, rub with rouge cloth. Or, to give the units the look of age, use liver of sulphur in water. It will darken the metal. Highlight parts later using a brush and polish or rouge cloth.

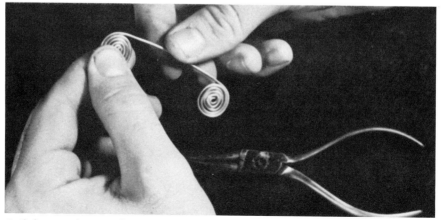

Coil the wire from each end, beginning with a small loop made with a fine round-nosed pliers. The wire must be wound tightly, until three inches of wire remains between the two coils.

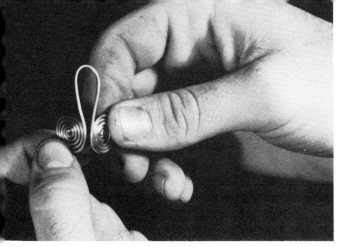

Bend the wire at its center to form a loop, making certain that both coils remain flat.

Then bend that loop back on itself. The links in the background are from an old Javanese belt; a soldered silver crossbar keeps the coils from ever unraveling.

Individual units are interlinked by slipping each loop through the next.

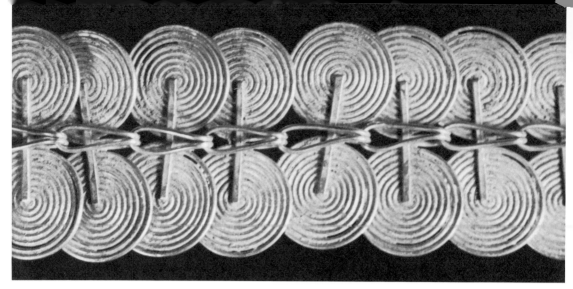

In the final form, all loops should lie flat, and the units should overlap slightly at regular intervals.

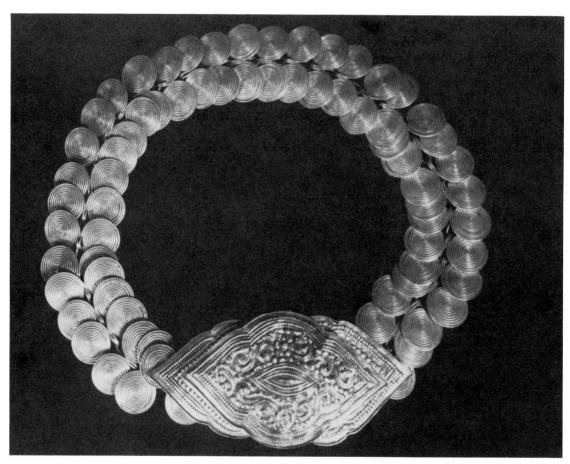

Coil belt with a chased silver buckle. Indonesia, circa 1875.

A bronze Greek fibula, circa 10th-8th century B.C. Courtesy: The Metropolitan Museum of Art, Fletcher Fund 1937.

ENAMELING WITH WIRE:
CLOISONNÉ AND PLIQUE-À-JOUR

Enameling, the use of powered glass in combination with metals, is an ancient technique, too. Finely powdered glass, applied to a metal surface, fuses to the metal when the piece is fired in a kiln. The process is repeated until the desired thickness and coloration have been achieved. The result: richly colored forms highlighted in wire.

Flat wires are used most often in *cloisonné* (from the French *cloison*, or "partition"). The wires are attached to the metal to partition areas and to create distinct divisions between glasses of different colors. Wire is also the basis of a more sophisticated and demanding enameling technique known as *plique-à-jour*. In plique-à-jour, enamel is contained solely by the flat wires—the cloisons without any metal backing. In this process, only fine transparent enamels are used, because much of the beauty of those pieces involves the transparency as light passes through the form. Of the two techniques, plique-à-jour is by far the more difficult, and, probably for that reason, cloisonné is practiced more often.

Enamels

Enamels come in three basic types: opaque, translucent, and transparent. Each type comes in a wide range of colors and degrees of fineness. Often, the color of the unfired enamel will be quite different from the fired glass. It is wise to fire sample pieces if color is crucial to a design. Enamels may be applied to the surfaces in dry form, or, in some applications, it may be convenient to barely saturate the powder with water. Many instruments may be used to apply the enamels. We have had great success with tools discarded by dentists. They come in a wide variety of shapes and some are particularly fine, making small sections (cloisons) easier to fill properly.

Fine enamels are quite expensive, especially certain precious colors. Therefore, it is wise to work over a piece of paper, so that spilled or overflowed enamels will not be lost. Marvelous colors and effects have been achieved by using the mixed color enamels that would otherwise be wasted. Impurities may always be removed—and should be removed—by straining the powdered glass.

Cloisonné

Cloisonné most often involves partitions made of flat metal wires. Cloisonné may be of gold, or silver, or copper—or some combination of the three in a single piece.

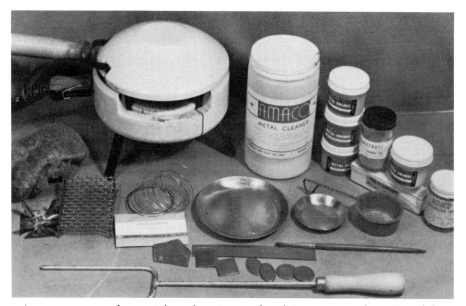

An arrangement of materials and equipment for cloisonné enameling. From left to right: steel wool, the enameling kiln, powdered concentrate metal cleaner (Amaco), a variety of transparent and opaque enamels, metal and wire trivets to hold the forms while in the kiln, silver and copper flat wire for making cloisons, a variety of copper forms, an enamel strainer, lavender oil, a kiln fork to place forms in the kiln and remove them onto the nichrome wire rack.

Attaching the Cloisons

Three methods may be used to attach the cloisons to the metal backing. Traditionally, they were soldered into place. But the cloisons may also **be** set into position by placing them in a solution of gum of tragacanth mixed to a gluelike consistency. After such placement, the gum is allowed to dry, and then the enamels are applied. The piece is fired, and the tragacanth burns off. A third technique, illustrated here, is probably easiest. The cloisons are placed on the prepared metal which has been coated with clear flux (uncolored enamel). The piece is then fired and the cloisons are held in place by that first thin layer of glass.

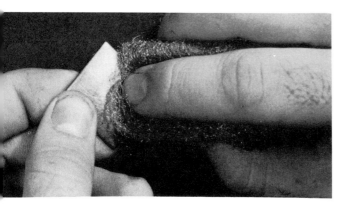

Enamels may be used on many metals, but since the base is usually hidden there is no advantage to using precious materials; copper is used most often. The metal must first be cleaned with steel wool; this removes surface dirt and also gives the metal "tooth."

To remove grease, soak the copper briefly in pickle or metal cleaner. Then rinse thoroughly with running water and pat dry.

Preparing the Metal

The metal, which can be purchased in a variety of shapes or by the sheet in craft and hobby and art stores, must be prepared before the cloisons are applied. Begin by rubbing the metal with steel wool. This cleans the metal and also gives it "tooth" so that the enamel will adhere properly. Both sides should be steelwooled, and the metal should be cleaned briefly in a sulphuric acid/water pickle or another metal cleaner such as Sparex[R] (see "Pickling" in Chapter 3). Cloisons should also be cleaned in the pickle or metal cleaner. Grease and dirt inhibit adhesion of the enamel.

Fastidious craftsmen will usually counterenamel the metal backing. This involves applying and firing a thin coat of enamel to the back surface of the form. Counterenameling prevents cracking due to uneven rates of contraction and expansion between metal and enamel.

Counterenameling also eliminates problems of scaling of metal which results from oxidation of the metal during heating and cooling. To prevent scaling in the absence of counterenameling, apply a coat of Scalex[R] (or other product meant for the same purpose) to the surfaces that are to be fired but not enameled. Such a scale preventative can be made by mixing white clay with water.

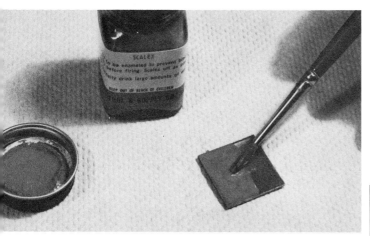

To prevent cracking due to differences in the contraction-expansion ratios, many enameled forms are counterenameled—that is to say, their backs are first given a coating of enamel. On this small form the process was shortened by eliminating that step, but to protect the back from excessive scaling due to the heat, the unenameled copper must be painted with a thin layer of clay-water or Scalex[R] before each firing.

Lavender oil (enameling oil) should be brushed onto the metal. It burns away quickly in the kiln and, in the meantime, holds the clear flux onto the form during the first firing.

A thin layer of clear flux should be sifted onto the oiled metal. In this case, the clear flux will provide a basis for further layers of enamel and also secure the cloisons.

Shaping the Cloisons

Cloisons may be made from almost any type of flat wire. Bend them with any type of pliers to the form required by the particular design. Keep the cloisons as flat to the plane of the metal as possible, since extreme unevenness will make it more difficult to attach them.

The cloisons may be large or small. Cloisons need not be closed, although most often they are. Open cloisons may be preferred in certain designs where a gradual shift in the color of the enamel will be expected. William Harper, for example, uses cloisons as accents in many pieces rather than solely as enclosures. The use of wire cloisons as decorative elements rather than as functional, structural units should not be overlooked.

Apply the finished cloisons to the metal with tweezers—after the wires have been cleaned and dried. If using the clear flux technique, set them down carefully. This method is explained more fully in the accompanying photographs and captions.

If soldering the cloisons, of course, the entire piece must be cleaned in pickle after that operation.

Applying the Enamels

Enamels may be filled into the cloisons by any convenient method. First, be certain to paint the surfaces not to be fired with an antiscaling substance. Then apply the powder. There are special tools for applying the enamels, but, as mentioned earlier, convenience is really the only requirement for the tools. Use utensils that are fine enough to do the job effectively —tweezers and dental instruments that dentists have discarded are often eminently usable.

The Heating Process

The metal form with filled cloisons is carefully set on a ceramic plate within an enameling kiln. Most such kilns are one-temperature units. They get *extremely* hot. Great care must be taken that the kiln does not rest upon or near flammable objects. If possible, a quarter-inch piece of asbestos should be used as a base for the small kiln. Metal spatulas make good table-to-kiln transferal instruments.

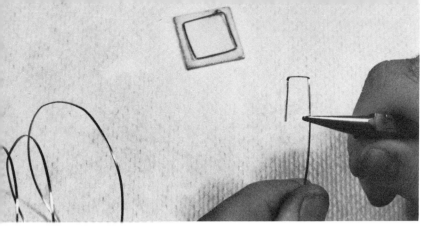

Bend the flat wire with smooth-jawed pliers. Cloisons must be as flat to the shape of the base as possible.

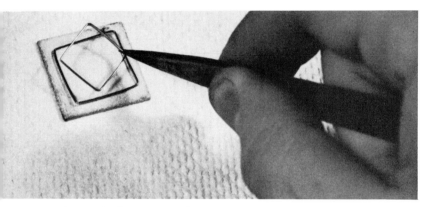

Set each element onto the flux, taking care not to unduly muss the clear flux.

With cloisons in place, the entire form is placed in the oven. When it is red hot and the powdered glass takes on a dull, even sheen it is ready to be removed. Never overheat enamels. When removed, the cloisons should be firmly set in the clear glass.

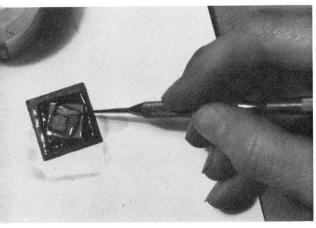

Colored enamels may then be placed within the cloisons. Dental tools make delicate and efficient working implements. Apply thin layers of the powders. This is a gradual process; the enamels within the cloisons must be built up slowly. Every time the piece is fired, the underside must also be painted with the antiscalant. That substance flakes away after firing.

To make certain that the enamel sticks to curved surfaces and edges, paint the area with enameling oil.

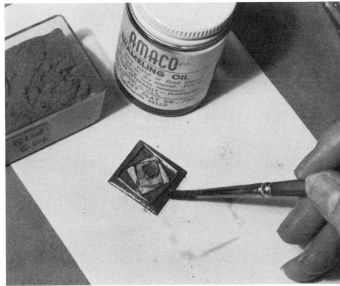

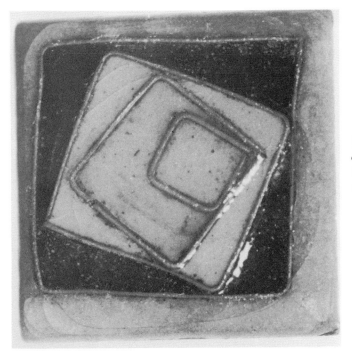

The final form was filed to clean each cloison and then given a final coating of clear flux. Enamels are often ground smooth with special stones.

A modern Japanese cloisonné pin.

Traditional kilns may also be used in enameling, although there is a great deal of convenience to the form and size of the smaller enameling kilns since it is very easy to peek in while the enamel is melting.

During the heating process, the glass powder first granulates, it gets red hot, and then appears to become flat and smooth. It is then that the layer has fused. The piece should be removed immediately after this occurs. The glass does flow, but only slightly, so do not allow the form to remain under the heat in the hope that each tiny crack and fillet of the cloisons will be filled in by slight overheating.

Always expect to fire a form several or many times. Enamels should not be applied thickly. Rather, many thin layers should be built up in successive firings. All enamels shrink, but because some enamels shrink more than others, different colors and qualities will sometimes require more attention and more layers than others. Unless absolutely impossible, always enamel the entire surface each time to prevent overfiring of any one area.

Never cool the enamels artificially by dipping the piece in water—the glass may crack.

Finishing

When the enamel reaches the level of the wires the enameling process is finished. Several treatments may be used to finish the form. Traditionally, the enameled form (if it is a small one) is set in heated pitch at the end of a stick ("dop stick") and ground smooth and fine on wet emery paper. Larger pieces may be sanded with the wet emery paper or ground with a stone made just for that purpose. But many craftsmen prefer an uneven texture. To finish the piece and keep that texture, clean the cloisons with emery paper or a file, coat the entire form with clear flux sifted on evenly, and fire the piece once more. This yields a fine, glossy surface.

The final object may be mounted in any way. Findings may be attached to pins, cuff links, and pendants by soldering or using plastic adhesives.

This piece by William Harper indicates that cloisonné can be an art form as well as a fine craft.

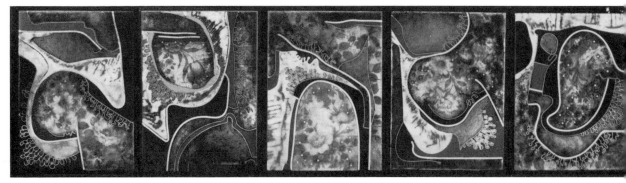

Scent Gardens (1973), by William Harper, gold and silver cloisonné enamel on
copper. Courtesy: William Harper, photograph by Evon Streetman.

William Harper's cloisonné enamels are ground to a smooth matte surface. This
piece consists of nine individual units, framed in Plexiglas.

A. Alan Perkins, on the other hand, allows his enamels to remain unpolished, intentionally filling cloisons to different heights. He uses fine silver cloisonné wire (1mm x .15mm) over silver or gold foil. Thin layers of transparent enamel allow the color of the underlying metal to show through. Courtesy: A. Alan Perkins.

Plique-à-jour

Plique-à-jour uses no backplate, and transparent enamels are invariably used. The design is sketched and translated into flat wire cloisons. The cloisons must then be soldered together—since they are the sole and complete support for the form and enamel.

It is important in plique-à-jour that the individual cloisons be small. In part this is to add strength. It also assures that even as the enamels shrink they will not shrink entirely away from the walls of the individual partitions. As with cloisonné, the level of the enamel must be built up slowly.

The soldered form is cleaned, dried, and placed upon a sheet of mica. The mica provides a smooth, hard surface for the enamel to melt and set against. Enamel is entered into the cloisons and fired as many times as necessary. After firing is completed, the mica is removed.

A panel of translucent glass contained by fine flat wires remains. Because of the brilliant, intense colors available in transparent enamels, the effect has often been likened to stained glass. The art of plique-à-jour requires consummate skill.

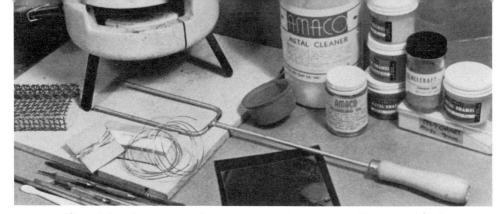

Plique à jour is a very sophisticated enameling process. The materials shown here are nearly the same as those used in cloisonné, except that only transparent enamels are used, and, rather than using a metal base, the fused glass is contained entirely by the metal wires. At the foreground is a piece of mica. The cloisons are placed on this surface and the piece is fired on the mica, too.

Plique-à-jour allows only the use of very fine cloisons, otherwise the enamels pull away from the wires because of shrinkage during firing. Usually, the cloisons are soldered to create a solid form with entirely closed sections. The flat wire must, in any case, be cleaned in a metal cleaner or pickle before filling with enamel.

An art nouveau butterfly pin in plique-à-jour. To achieve a smooth, matte finish, each side is finely ground after the cloisons have been filled.

PLASTIC PLIQUE-À-JOUR

Plique-à-jour is an elusive and difficult technique. With plastics, however, the same results are not only feasible, but easily achieved. The transparency of plastics such as polyester resin and the epoxies far exceeds that of glass, and technical restraints—such as having to make only small cloisons—are virtually eliminated.

The cloisons may be prepared in the same manner as is traditionally used with plique-à-jour, but, again, plastic has revolutionized the technique. Although it may still be desirable to solder individual cloisons, it is not necessary to create a solid, complete unit. Rather, the individual units are filled with a thin layer of clear plastic resin. The self-contained piece—with individual units suspended within by a thin sheet of clear plastic—remains to be filled with colored resins.

The work may be conducted on a sheet of Mylar[R], or on glass that has been coated with silicone or sprayed with wax (Johnson's Pledge[R] works well). It *is* important to have a smooth, clean, and flat working surface, because this is precisely the surface that will be reproduced on the object by the plastic.

The outlining cloison is placed on the working surface and dammed all around its outside edge with a plastic putty or clay. This will prevent the resin from seeping out. A thin layer of clear, uncolored resin is poured inside the cloison. Any inner cloisons are then carefully placed into the still liquid resin. This resin layer cures in one to five hours depending on resin and catalyst (see below), producing a leakproof reservoir. The cloisons, now sealed at the base with clear plastic, are ready to accept a layer of colored resin. Although one must wait longer for layers to cure when working with plastic as opposed to glass, only two or three fillings will be required in most applications, compared with the often tedious number of fillings and refirings necessary in the glass process.

If the metal cloisons have been soldered to create completely closed areas, it will be possible to fill all the spaces at once in any number of colors. But if cloisons have cracks or are allowed to remain open, each must be plugged with a small piece of putty before each filling to avoid leaking colored resin into the neighboring cloisons. Necessarily, each must be filled individually. Do not wait until the sections are completely cured to begin filling the next. Once the plastic has *gelled* it will not flow into other sections. Remove the putty and fill the next cloison.

The two logical materials for plastic plique-à-jour are polyester resin (boat resin) and epoxy resin. Of the two, epoxies are superior because shrinkage is negligible and they degrade much less rapidly. Use clear, water-white epoxy whenever possible.

Both materials are sirupy liquids and require the addition of a catalyst in order to "cure" or harden into a solid state. The materials are accompanied by instructions explaining the proper proportion of catalyst to resin. Usually, those recommendations are for average casting thicknesses. Because more heat is wasted by the thin castings used in plastic plique-à-jour, the amounts of catalyst used should be increased slightly.

Proportions of catalyst to polyester and epoxy resin in thin castings are included here as a general guide. The polyester proportions are based on use of Reichold Chemical Company's Polylite 32-032 resin. The epoxy proportions are in reference to different catalysts used in conjunction with 100 grams of Ciba Company's Epoxy Araldite 502 resin.

THIN CASTINGS OF POLYESTER RESIN	
Polyester Resin	*MEK Peroxide Catalyst*
2 tablespoons (1 oz.)	20 drops
6 tablespoons (3 oz.)	¼ teaspoon
1 cup (8 oz.)	½ teaspoon
1 pint (2 cups)	1¼ teaspoons

THIN CASTINGS OF EPOXY RESINS		
Curing Agent	*Amount by Weight (in grams)*	*Curing Time*
RC125 (Jones-Dabney Co. #87)	50	20 min.
956 (Ciba Company)	20	1–3 hrs.
B-001 (Ajinomoto Company, Inc.)	50	1 hour

Reproduced Courtesy Thelma R. Newman, *Plastics As Craft*

Colorants should be added to the resin before catalyzation. A variety of commercial pigments available in powder, paste, and liquid forms may be used. As in enameling, these pigments are transparent, translucent, or opaque.

Modern technology has made it possible to capture the beauty of plique-à-jour more easily. Metal cloisons may be filled with epoxy and polyester resins in brilliant, transparent colors. The materials shown here include a pin board to form and shape the flat metal wire, a propane torch and different grades of solder, a metal snips, a jeweler's saw, files, and pickle solution.

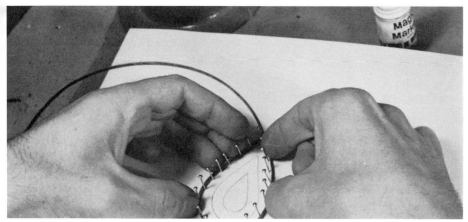

Flat silver wire is bent around metal pins stuck into cardboard. The pins approximate the precise shape desired. The pencil lines within will later be "pinned" and wire will be shaped around them as well.

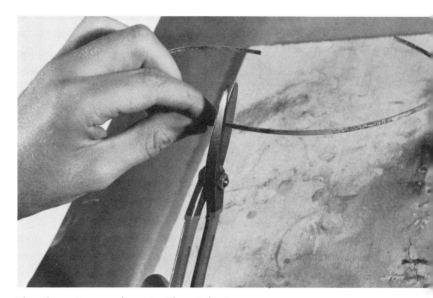

The silver wire may be cut with metal snips . . .

. . . or with a jeweler's saw. While the hand snips are the faster route, speed is deceptive, since the snipped ends must then be . . .

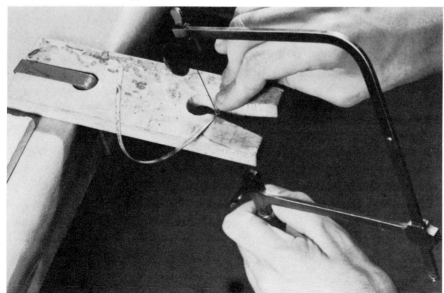

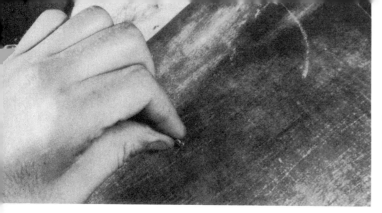

. . . sanded until they are perfectly smooth and flat, the natural result from sawing.

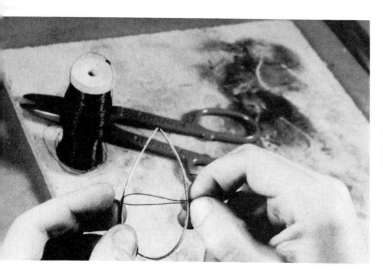

In preparation for soldering, the ends of this cloison are held together with iron binding wire. The soldering process is illustrated in chapter 3.

After soldering, the inside of this cloison is sanded to give it some tooth. The additional roughness enables the plastic resin to adhere more readily.

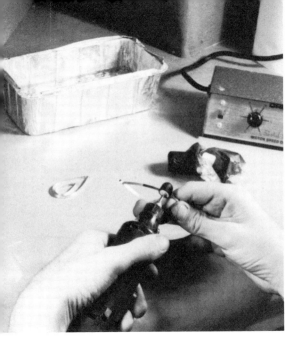

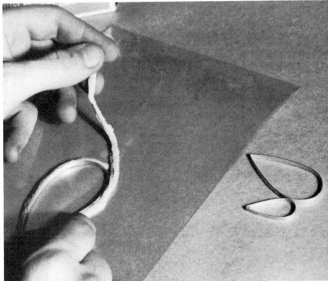

The exposed outside is polished to a high gloss.

When each cloison has been soldered, the outer form is placed on a piece of Mylar^R film, polyethylene film, or waxed paper. Dam the form with plastic putty or clay to prevent leakage. While the outside of the largest cloison was polished, the inside and outside of the other pieces have been sanded slightly.

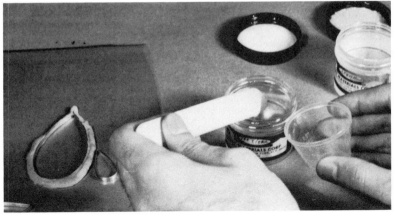

Epoxy is a very effective filler because shrinkage is minimal. Mix the resin and catalyst in a plastic cup. Some resin systems require weight measurement, others need only volume proportioning. Catalyst, usually added in small quantities, may be fed in with an eyedropper.

A thin layer of uncolored resin will set the cloisons in position. Pour in enough epoxy to fill the area only one-third of the way.

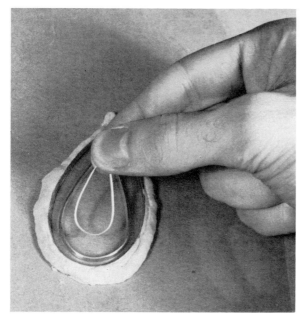

Place the inner cloisons in position.

The form may be weighted to hold the cloisons in place while the plastic cures.

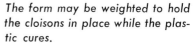

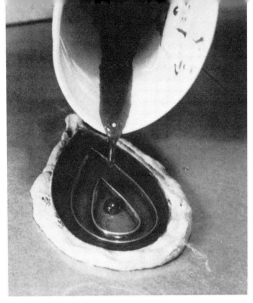

When the uncolored layer gels, colored epoxy may be poured into each section. Mix the epoxy the same way, adding transparent color. Fill to the top, but not to overflowing.

Occasional runovers may result if the table is not level. Use paper or tongue depressors inserted beneath the form to keep it level, and use cotton swabs to remove excess or spilled resin.

Plastic plique-à-jour offers many advantages over the traditional method. In forms like this one, for example, the cloisons need not be a single unit, and there is almost no investment in equipment like enamels and a firing kiln. The range of colors is extraordinary too.

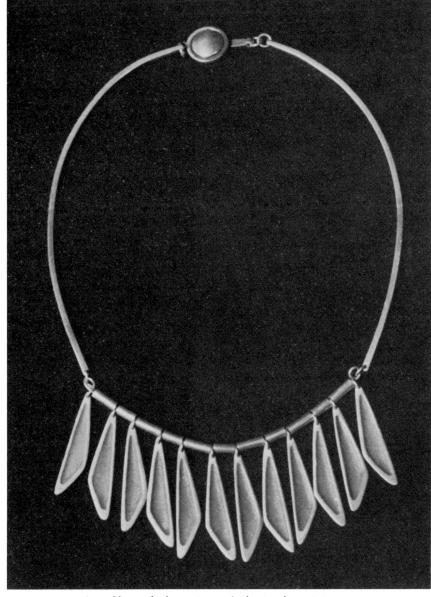

A necklace of silver wire and plastic plique-à-jour.

WIRE EMBEDMENTS IN EPOXY

Wire and clear two-part epoxy can be combined to create hard, waterproof decorations for many surfaces.

Bend a soft brass wire (30-gauge is used here) into any two-dimensional design that will fit on the surface to be decorated. Wood surfaces will best accept the epoxy resin, but plastics and some untreated metals will work well, too. The wire may be applied as it is, or it may be forged in part or whole.

Thoroughly mix enough two-part epoxy adhesive (available in hardware stores) to cover the surface thinly. For this first step, one of the quick-hardening five- or ten-minute epoxies would be helpful. Apply the resin to the surface with a stick, spatula, or tongue depressor and quickly press the wire design into the adhesive. The fast-drying epoxies require that the work be done quickly. When the first layer has nearly hardened, apply an additional layer of epoxy. As many layers as are desired may be spread over each earlier coating. Just be certain that each layer dries first and that the epoxy coats the surface evenly. After several levels have been built up, use sandpaper to remove any lumpiness, and carefully apply a final layer of epoxy to fill in any remaining gaps and eliminate sanding lines.

DECORATIVE BOX

Epoxies may be used to embed wire forms as well. Begin by bending wire to shape and hammering it out.

Prepare a box by painting it with acrylic paint. Allow the paint to dry thoroughly.

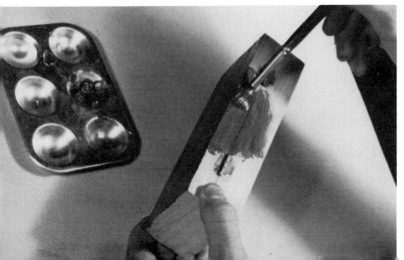

Spread a thin layer of quick-hardening epoxy adhesive over the surface to be decorated. The epoxy shown here comes in Siamese tubes —one squeeze produces equal amounts of resin and catalyst.

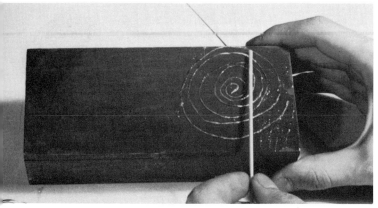

Work quickly because the epoxy sets rapidly. Press the beaten wire into the epoxy. The wire elements must be stuck down securely.

Mix more epoxy and cover the entire surface in one smooth coat. If wires persist in protruding, apply one or two more coatings, and sand the surface between applications to eliminate unevenness.

The box.

A Japanese sword guard with inlaid gold wire and mother-of-pearl (3″ x 2 3/4″).
Courtesy: The Metropolitan Museum of Art, Havemeyer Bequest, 1929.

FILIGREE

Filigree is another process that has been popular around the world for centuries. Filigree remains one of the most delicate applications of wire, producing intricate lacelike forms in metal.

Fine silver is typically used in filigree. Once annealed, the fine silver wire is easily shaped into the characteristic ovals, scrolls, coils, and circles of the art. Naturalistic and geometric designs are most common. Flat wire and wire that has been twisted and then hammered flat are most often used in filigree, although other shapes of wire—some formed using a drawplate—have applications as well.

The filigree worker makes an outer framework for each filigree unit. Fashioned in heavier wire, the framework defines the area to be filled with the finer wire. The larger framework must be subdivided into smaller units with the same heavier wire. The framework and subdivisions are hard-soldered together.

Having thus defined the filigree spaces, swirls and twists of fine wire are made with fine-pointed pliers and deft hands. Each space in the design is filled quite tightly, allowing no movement within the frame. The fill-in designs, as well as larger units, must all fit so that they touch—otherwise soldering will be ineffective.

To solder the filigree, make a solder-flux powder. File the edge of an easy solder sheet to produce fine granules of easy solder. Mix the bits of solder with borax powder (flux) in a ratio of 10 to 1. Spread the mixture over the entire filigree. The softest possible flame must be used to avoid overheating and melting the fine wires. For most filigree work, the heat should come from *below,* so that the solder will flow toward the heat and between the wires. Place the filigree on a sheet of mica and then on a ring stand, and heat from underneath. This allows more even heating of the entire piece. As soon as the solder flows, remove the heat. Additional soldering may be necessary, but pickle the filigree after each soldering, otherwise the borax and oxides may interfere.

Filigree begins with a larger framework. Convenient subdivisions are filled with coils and swirls of fine wire in a repeat design. Most artisans construct the outer framework of heavier wire and hard solder it.

Filigree units are usually thin and flat, but by stacking and soldering layers, three-dimensional reliefs are formed. To protect soldered areas, paint them with yellow ochre or powdered rouge inhibiting-paste. Always be careful not to get paste on the parts to be soldered After soldering, remove the paste with a stiff brush and water. Never pickle a piece that has the inhibitory paste on it—this contaminates the pickle solution.

To flatten filigree, use a hard rubber mallet or wood mallet. To curve filigree units, shape over wooden molds using the same mallet.

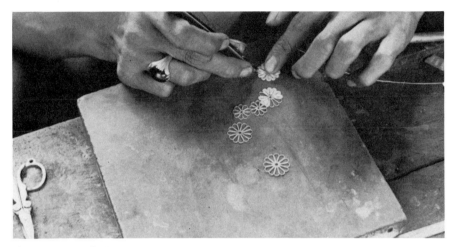

This artisan coils fine silver wire by hand, with tweezers and with pliers. He then bends the flat coil and fits it into a section of the filigree framework. It must fit perfectly, with no play.

In keeping with Southeast Asian practice, the piece is then soaked in a mixture of water and borax. This cleans and fluxes the form.

After soaking in flux solution, the piece is removed and sprinkled with a powder of soft solder. The artist holds the form with tweezers so that the solder may be applied evenly to the entire surface; this also prevents grease deposits from fingers.

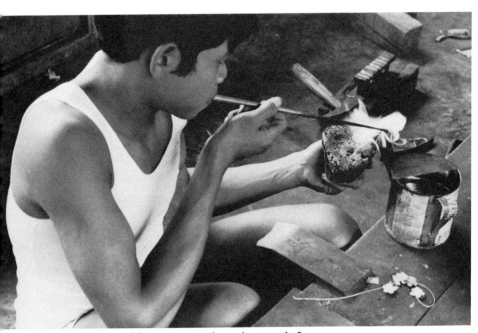

A blowpipe provides a large soft flame.

A 19th-century filigree pendant from Spain.

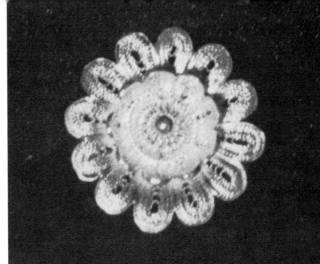

Several filigree elements were hammered into curved shapes over a wooden mold and combined in a ring.

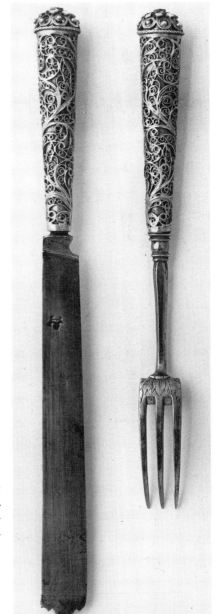

Filigree knife and fork in silver gilt. Germany, 1660–70. Courtesy: Museum of Decorative Art, Copenhagen.

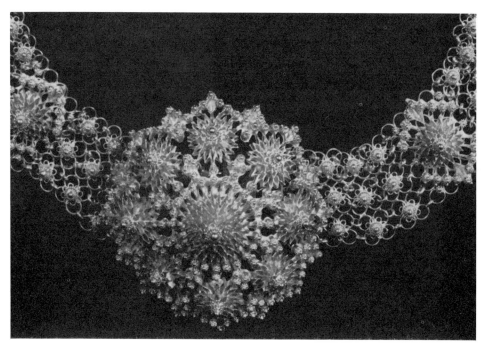

A belt and buckle of fine filigree wire from
southern Thailand.

WIRE EMBEDMENTS IN FUSIBLE PLASTICS

Wire embedded in fusible plastic offers great possibilities for the creation of colorful ornaments and window hangings.

Plastic tiles, like Poly-Mosaics^R, melt and fuse safely in a home oven or broiler oven at 350°F. Arrange the Poly-Mosaics on a cookie sheet so that their edges touch. The tiles may be used whole, or they may be cut easily with tile nippers, large nail clippers, or with the tap of chisel and hammer. The tiles are nontoxic, but should nonetheless be used in a well-ventilated area. Melt the tiles in an oven for just a few minutes until their edges begin to soften and the tiles begin to fuse together. Remove them from the oven, and while still hot, press wire into the plastic.

Allow the length of wire to extend beyond the plastic forms so that hanging loops may be bent later. Set half, cut, or whole Poly-Mosaic tiles over the wire, sandwiching the wire. Place the cookie sheet—wire and all—back in the oven. Heat the plastic again until the newly applied top tiles fuse to the bottom layer. The plastic may be straightened or otherwise manipulated by momentarily removing the forms from the oven and pressing, pushing, and flattening the hot material with a metal spatula.

When the plastic tiles have fused securely around the wires, remove the forms from the oven and allow them to cool. Texture may be varied considerably by adding more or less plastic and heating for varying lengths of time.

Twist loops in the ends of the wires and string them over a wire frame. Only fitting that a plastic material like wire will be combined with a medium equally plastic!

Place Poly-Mosaic^R tiles on an aluminum cookie sheet for fusing.

These colorful plastic tiles may be cut easily. Use tile nippers, large nail clippers—or even a chisel and hammer. When the tiles have been arranged, place the cookie sheet in an oven or broiler oven at 350°F. The tiles fuse in three to five minutes. The longer they remain under the heat, the more they will melt. Only fuse the tiles slightly.

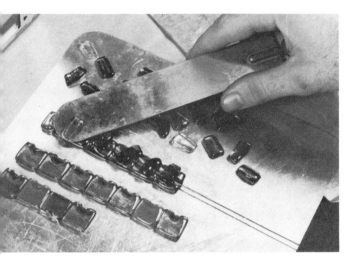

Heat a number of half-tiles at the same time. Remove the tray from the oven and add wire stems by sandwiching them between partially fused/melted Poly-Mosaics. Return the tiles to the oven until they fuse together firmly around the wires.

After removing the stemmed forms, "polish" the backs with a soft flame from a propane torch.

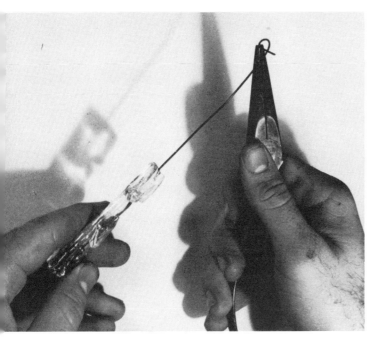

Make a loop in each stem . . .

. . . and hang the lot from a wire framework.

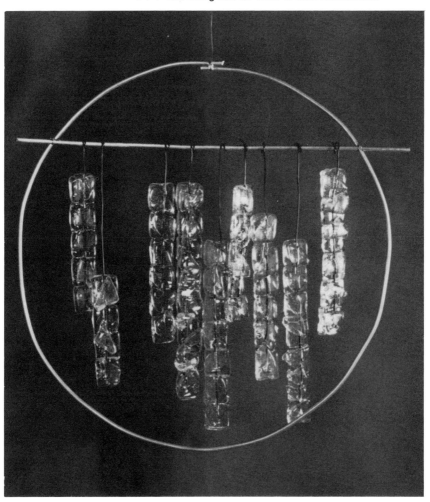

GRAPHIC EFFECTS IN WIRE

Wire may be used to create complex linear forms. Sue Fuller is the recognized master of this technique. Using fine plastic and fiber lines she developed complex patterns involving many layers and subtle variations in color. The same effects may be achieved with wire—or using wire in combination with other materials like yarns of different colors and textures, or plastic lines.

The basic method is quite simple. The wire must be strung around points that stand in some symmetrical relationship to one another. The symmetry need not be a familiar one, nor need it be "regular." The only requirement is that there be some systematic correspondence among points. In this illustration, three rows of nails were arranged on composition board. Each row contains exactly the same number of nails. Beginning at the end of one row, the wire was tied and then stretched to the corresponding end nail on the next row, then stretched onto the first nail of the third row—but, then, the wire is stretched to the *second* nail of the original row, and so on down the line. What this effectively does is to shift the axis of the triangle we are creating. This achieves the desired appearance of many triangles overlapping in a single plane, or, if you will, a single triangle rotating in that same plane.

Different symmographic effects can be achieved by varying the relationships and spacings of the pivotal elements (the nails). Even within the same pattern, different results are possible by varying the amount by which the triangle shifts. To do that, one might consider moving to the *third* nail rather than moving directly to the second, thereby consistently skipping one nail each time.

Similar effects can be achieved three-dimensionally, defining volumes in space. By using a framework covered with aluminum screening, wires attached in sequence can readily be used to suggest volumes—like the cones in this example. This idea may be extended, too, because if the framework were in a box with screening on every side there should be no obstacle to creating every form of regular and irregular geometric structure within that box—using only individual wires as definitional elements. With great patience, one could even approximate a circle.

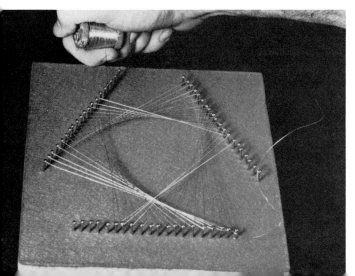

Beginning with the first nail in any row, wrap the wire end securely around the nail. Then stretch the wire to the corresponding "first" nail in the next row, and then to the "first" nail in the third row. To shift the triangle, proceed to stretch the wire to the "second" nails in series. Move on to the "third" nails, and so forth, until the last nail has been strung.

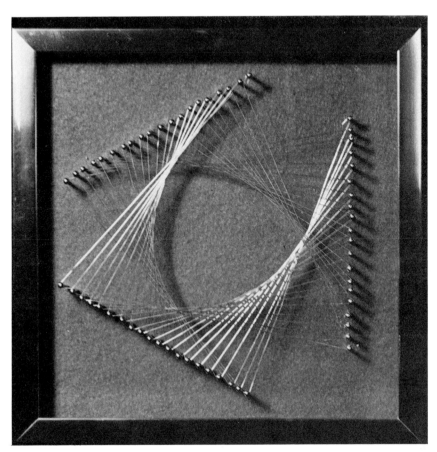

Although we chose a regular form, this technique may be used to create an end-less variety of wire graphics. The only requirement is that there be some functional relationship between the nails. In a circle, for example, one would need to establish the number of nails skipped during each stretch of wire. The number of that shift would determine the resulting design. Once the wire has been wrapped around, it becomes difficult to reuse. Experiment with string, which may be rewound and reused many times. Try creating graphics using different colors of wire. The possibilities are truly infinite, since the areas being defined are limited only by the number of points in a plane.

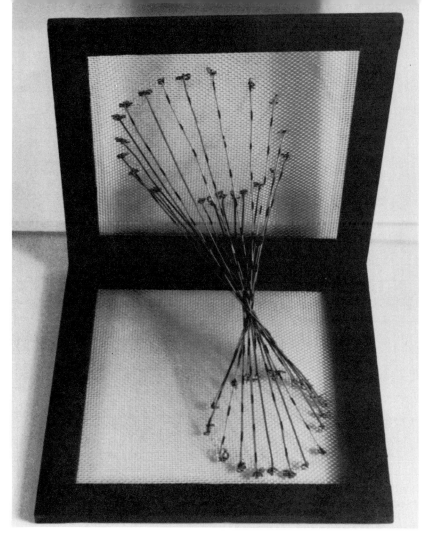

Similar effects may be achieved three-dimensionally. Screening was stapled to the back of a pine framework which had been painted black. Colorfully insulated telephone wires were then inserted in series to define mirroring cones in space. More complex structures may be built in a box frame covered on six sides with screening.

WIRE EMBROIDERY

Flat and round wires can be embroidered very attractively onto diverse materials. All that is needed is the wire, the material (in this case, leather), a design idea, a shears to cut the wire, and a hole punch of some sort. Silver wire was often used to embroider objects for African nobles. The idea is distantly related to the Indian sari woven with the finest gold threads.

A more modern and perhaps more natural adaptation is embroidery of wire through screening. Aluminum or steel screening—the kind used to keep the bugs out—is, after all, interwoven wire. The space in the weave is just enough to pass thin wires through. Telephone wire—copper-insulated by colorful plastic sheaths—offers ample variety for wire/screen embroidery. Most stitches used in regular embroidery can be translated readily into wire.

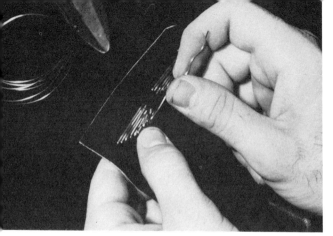

To embroider with flat or round wires, first pierce
the material at the points of insertion. This becomes especially important with dense materials
like leather. Here, flat silver cloisonné wire is
being passed through holes punched in leather
with an awl.

Koran case of leather embroidered in silver, lamellé, in the so-called
Hispano-Moresque style of the 15th century. It bears the device
of the kings of Granada, suggesting that it probably belonged to
Mohammed Abu Abdullah, the last Moorish king of Granada. Courtesy: The Metropolitan Museum of Art, Rogers Fund, 1904.

The Zulu embroider small gourds like this one (3″ diameter) as containers for snuff or medicine. Courtesy: Smithsonian Institution.

Like the grid cloth used in needlepoint, wire screening makes a perfect background for wire embroidery. Flexible, insulated copper wire may not only be worked in all embroidery stitches, but it is nearly as variously colorful as thread.

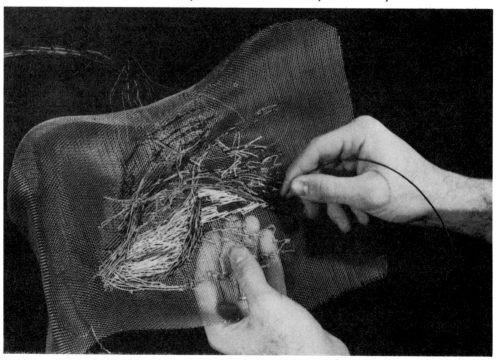

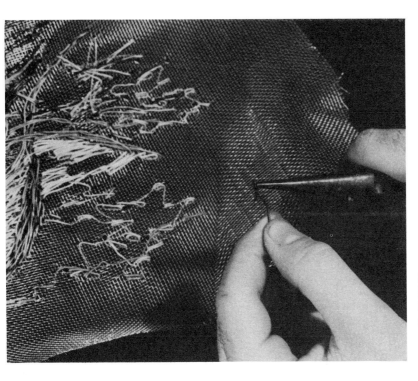

Secure single strands with pliers by making tiny knots at the back. This is also a good way to make French knots.

Wire flames in flashing colors.

SCREEN WEAVING

Wire can be woven into screening directly if it is fine enough. Otherwise, remove strands of screening wire and replace them with different wire strands. The lengths of screening wire are pulled out with fine pliers. Experiment by weaving wires of different colors, shapes, and thicknesses into the prepared screen. Experiment, too, with different weaves, and with different colors and shapes of aluminum and even plastic screens.

Remove strands of screening wire to make room for wires to be interwoven.

Wires of different gauges and colors may be woven into the screening. Single strands of heavy wire may fill a row, or many strands of fine wires may be used to fill sections at a time.

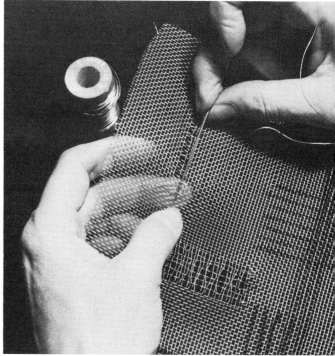

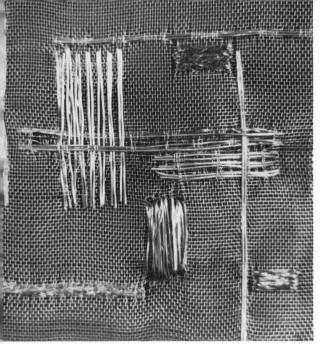

This technique suits angular designs, and patterns that depend upon significant division of space.

Two examples of fine screening wire woven around flat wire.

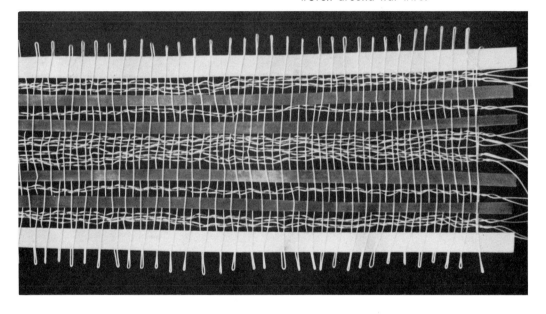

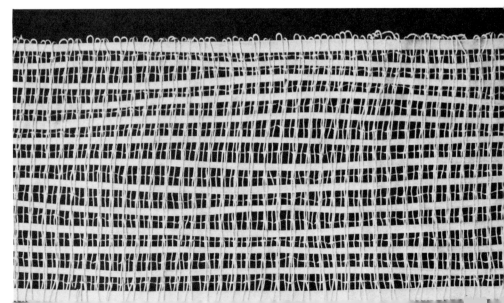

WIRE COLLAGE

With an assortment of screening—which comes in innumerable colors and densities of mesh—a wire collage can be assembled. Cut the screening with a shears, arrange the mesh, and "sew" the parts together with thin wire or "invisible" nylon thread. Manuel Rivera effectively combines wire mesh with twisted wire and a background of painted wood for dramatic textural effects.

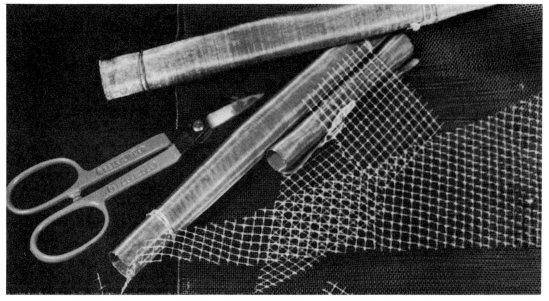

Screening is available in an incredible variety of grades and colors—from the coarsest chicken wire or carpenter's cloth to window screening and fine copper and brass wire mesh. Hardware stores often offer great bounties of used screening during the spring when they repair summer screens. For collage work, small, odd pieces are very often useful; it is wise to keep a scrap box for future use.

Cut screening to shape with wire shears. . .

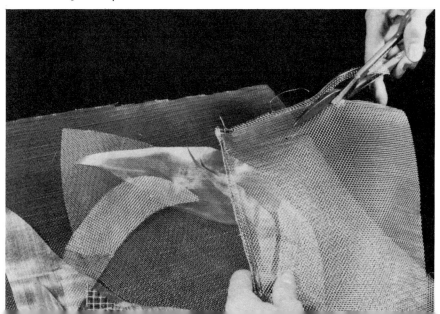

. . . and lace the pieces together with very thin pieces of wire or invisible nylon thread.

Wire and screen collage.

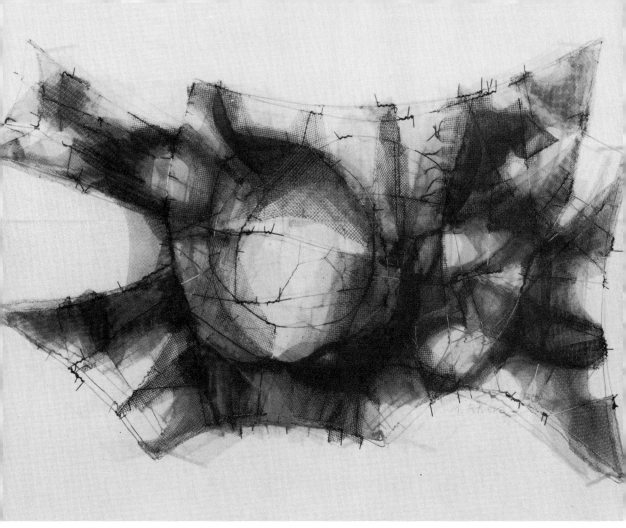

Metamorphosis (Blason) (1960, 32 1/4" x 40"), by Manuel Rivera, relief of wire mesh and wire on painted wood. Collection of The Museum of Modern Art, gift of Mr. and Mrs. Richard Rodgers.

MOVING OUT OF THE PLANE

The preceding applications involving screening suggests the obvious step from two to three dimensions in utilizing wire's full potential. With only shears and binding wire, screening, carpenter's cloth, or chicken wire becomes valuable structural material. The weave of screening is attractive when bent, because of the warped optical qualities created by the stretched weave. Screening can also be scored with a knife or other blunt instrument, or folded by hand alone to yield handsome repeat designs. Mesh has a character all its own. When combined with wire, the sensation of metal line with metal plane is exciting, as the work of Günter Haese illustrates.

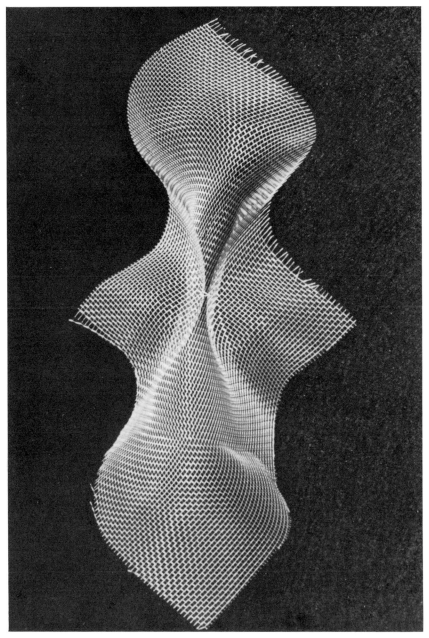

It is only natural to think of working screening three-dimensionally as well. Form it with fingers and stitch it at a point or two with a piece of wire.

Screening may be scored and bent as well. Use a dull knife to crease the fabric, or bend it along the edge of a table or board.

Double-scoring created this effect.

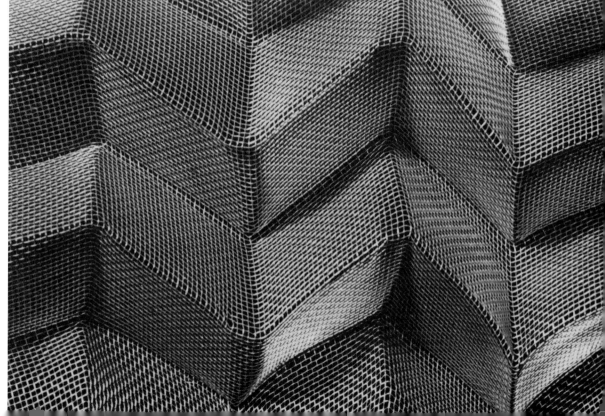

Children on the Beach (1940, 24 1/2" high), by Toni Hughes, constructed of plumber's hanger iron, galvanized wire cloth, screening, and various ornaments. Collection of *The Museum of Modern Art*.

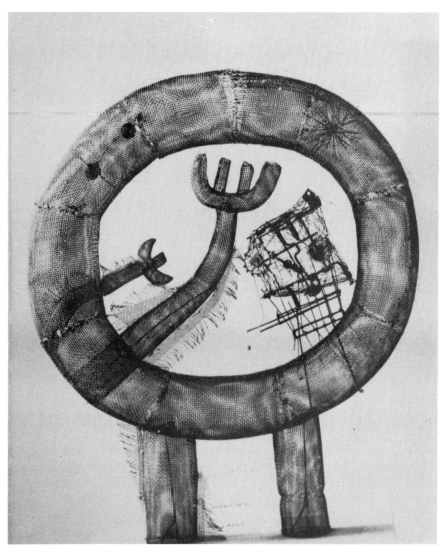

Seltene Kaktusart (1963, 12″ x 9″ x 3″), by Günter Haese, illustrates the artist's masterful use of wire screening.

Ganges (1968, 18″ x 9″ x 9″), by Günter **Haese**.

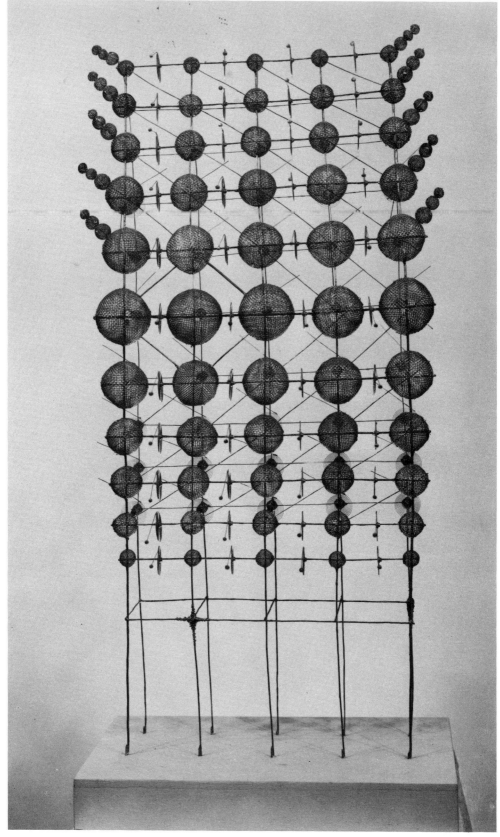

In Tibet (1964, 20″ x 9″), by Günter Haese, construction of clockwork parts, brass screening, and wire. Collection of The Museum of Modern Art, Blanchette Rockefeller Fund.

Chapter 5

WAX WIRE: LOST-WAX CASTING

The lost-wax casting process (*cire perdue*) is more than four thousand years old. Our earliest known examples come from Egypt (2690–2280 B.C.), but there appears to have been simultaneity in the development of the process without any core of communication. In Mesopotamia, Egypt, India, Luristan, China, and Africa there were trade connections for passing the skill, but in isolated pre-Columbian South America lost-wax casting was also a practiced art. We see continued development throughout history— the Greeks and Romans were skilled in the craft. Their traders and, later, French and Portuguese explorers brought these techniques with them to their colonies. Curiously, even though lost-wax was very popular as a sculpture-casting technique, the New World did not learn the ancient method of casting until the 1900s, when Riccardo Bertelli brought his skill to America from Italy.

Today the art of lost-wax casting is practiced in every part of the world, although the techniques and material vary from culture to culture. The western, industrialized nations have developed it into a fine, precise, even scientific process. But as illustrated below, the process itself is beautifully simple, and in many parts of the world lost-wax castings are finely and skillfully executed with minimal materials and makeshift tools.

The process essentially involves the creation of a model in wax. The wax is *invested,* or contained, within a shell of clay, charcoal, plaster, or some combination of those materials. The wax may then be melted out and metal poured into the space created within the *investment*. When the metal cools enough to lose its cherry color, the investment is placed in a bucket of water. This cools the piece, and, since the investment is still very hot, it also causes the investment to crack away from the casting.

WAX WIRE

The wax wires used by artisans are very often of the same material used by dentists. Called dental wax, it is usually a medium-hard wax that does not melt at body temperature. This quality makes it easier to work with since it usually will not get as sticky and gummy as waxes with lower melting temperatures. Some wax wires are, of course, made of wax that melts at lower temperatures. And all waxes may be used in combination—either with other wax wires or with sheet and block wax.

Wax wires are available commercially in many shapes including square, round, and triangular wires of assorted diameters. Flat wire can be made by cutting strips of wax from sheets with a razor blade. Or, for that matter, wax wires of more complex shapes can be made by making molds and pouring wax into those forms—a simple but time-consuming process, considering the variety of wax wires that are readily available.

Wax wires are available in different lengths, gauges, hardnesses, and shapes. Hardnesses range from wires made out of wax/plastic compositions that may be worked with chisels and metalworking tools, to beeswax wires that soften upon touching.

Maurice Abramson uses a fine-point heating pen to melt and shape wax, but equally effective tools are easily made. One device is a needle, its blunt end embedded in a cork. Simply heat the point in a candle flame and apply it to the wax. Dental tools may also be heated in a flame and applied to wax wires to shape them. Mr. Abramson here demonstrates his technique for making fine wax balls from a wax chunk or wax wire. He collects wax on the end of the heat point until there is so much that it falls off. The wax cools while falling, and may then be easily removed from the empty film canister. Different shapes may be achieved by dropping the wax from different heights: high drops will generally result in spheroids, since the wax has time to cool; drops from lower levels will result in half-rounds or, perhaps, flat blobs.

Most wax wires soften with the application of body heat from hands and fingers. This coil begins a pin of wax wire which will then be cast in gold.

Trim excesses of wax wire with a warm—not hot—single-edge razor blade.

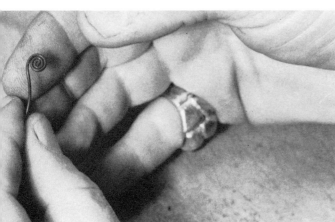

Maurice Abramson "tacks" the back side of the form by melting the wires together at several spots. The small dots will appear in the final object, but since they will be on the back—and since they are so very small—they will not be noticeable. If necessary, they may be filed away from the cast piece.

The wax may be shaped over any form. Metal shapes work well because the wax will separate from them easily.

The final form, constructed entirely of wax wires that were bent, tacked, and textured, also provided for the setting of the stones. Figure on shrinkage of 8 to 10 percent when considering settings and ring sizes.

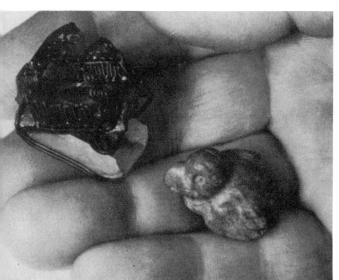

This setting was designed around a tiny pre-Columbian bird.

The wax form was constructed around a square mandrel, since Mr. Abramson wanted to create a square band. Mandrels make excellent working surfaces because they provide an exact size for the ring and help to maintain the correct shape. Mandrels come in many shapes, and are usually of graduating sizes.

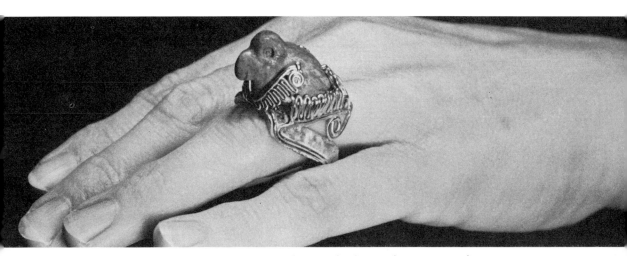

The cast bird cage by Maurice Abramson.

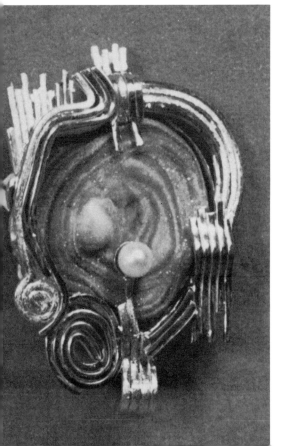

The curling strands of metal echo pearl and chalcedony shapes in this pin by Maurice Abramson.

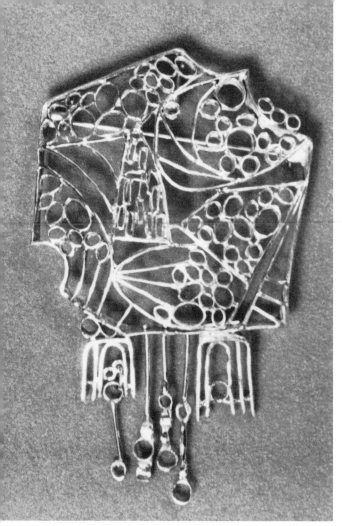

Many other materials besides wax may be used in casting models. Abramson hit upon the genius idea of using slides from ordinary drinking straws in combination with wax wires. The circular cross sections in this piece were all cut from straws of different sizes. When heated, the plastic melts out of the investment as cleanly as does the wax.

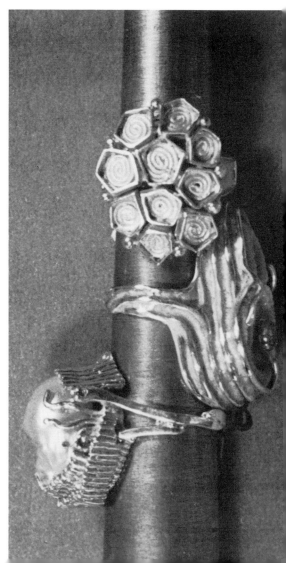

Very often, Maurice Abramson combines wax wire with pieces of wax cut or carved from solid blocks. And sometimes, too, he consciously melts together individual wires so that very solid forms result.

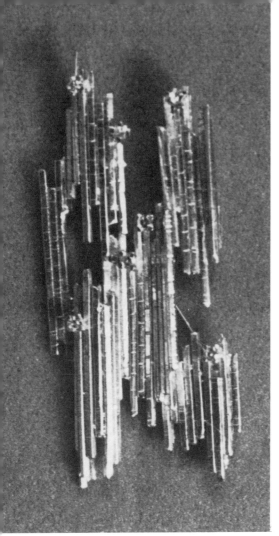

One beauty of wax is that it accepts texture so well. In this pin, Mr. Abramson textured square wax wires with a heated dental tool. Different waxes accept texture and detail in different degrees. The harder substances will allow very fine detail work; softer wax cannot be worked so accurately.

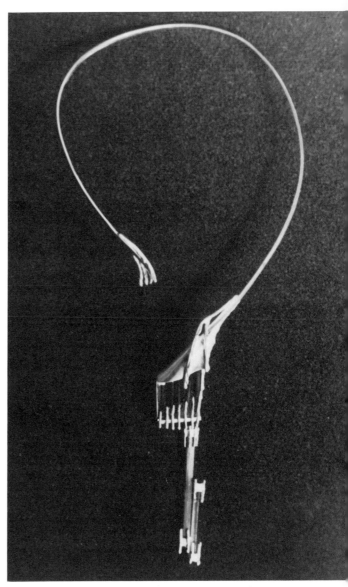

Necklace in the lost-wax casting process, from wax wire and sheet, by Maurice Abramson.

Working Wax Wire

All wax wire may be softened enough with body heat in order to form it. For that reason, wax wire is best worked by hand. By holding and kneading the wires we not only begin to define the form desired, but also soften the material into a workable consistency.

Some waxes hand-soften enough to be stuck together with little heat; they will not require further attachment to remain in the position given them. Other waxes, like dental wax wires, will require further melting to attach them.

A contemporary casting from wax wire of an ancient Mixtec thumb ring from Oaxaca, Mexico.

The device commonly used to effect that attachment is a heating pen with a very fine point. This inexpensive instrument melts the wax at the point of attachment. The degree of melting depends entirely upon the intention of the craftsman. Most pens have temperature controls and become hot enough to melt the wax entirely. Only a light touch with the pen tip will create a tiny, solderlike dot attachment. A makeshift heating pen can also be composed of a pin or needle embedded in a cork. The cork serves as a handle, and the tip of the pin picks up heat in a few seconds from candle flame or alcohol lamp. Wax does not require much in the way of such reinforcement. Wax wire tipped into a flame forms a natural ball or head—a fine punctuation to a line.

Every craftsman and artist develops little aids in working with wax. Creating volumes often demands molds. Maurice Abramson shapes wax over pieces of wood or lead. He connects the wires over the form and then removes the completed wax structure.

Many tools are valuable in working wax wires. Dental tools, because of their fineness, are of particular use. Fine tools can be passed through a candle flame and then used instead of a heating pen to join wax parts. A razor blade is essential to achieve clean, sharp cuts. For most purposes, too, a razor blade heated in a candle flame could be used to join wax parts.

Wax is the original plastic material. Nearly any form can be duplicated with it, and any number of working elements can be made from the basic wax wire. Twisted, crimped, stretched, bent, and coiled wires are the first to come to mind. Wax balls may also be made easily from the wire. By completely melting wax, taking it onto the tip of the pen point, and then shaking off a wax drop, a small ball of wax can be created. The falling drop cools in midair. If dropped from a low level, so that the wax hits while it is still molten, a half-sphere will be formed. Such elements make excellent surface treatments.

Preparing for Casting

After the wax original has been constructed it must be prepared for casting by the addition of the sprues and vents. The molten metal will flow through the sprue. Vents allow gases to escape during the heating of the investment and while the metal is being poured into the mold.

Sprue and vents are round wax wires that extend away from the wax form, and at the end of the sprue a funnellike piece of wax is attached to provide a larger area through which to pour the hot metal.

With vents and sprue in place, the entire form is painted with a debubblizer. This substance prevents bubbles from forming on the surface of the piece during casting, and also helps the investment to adhere to the wax original. In practice, sprue and vents are added to the form by the professional casters who do the bulk of this work.

The Casting Process

The investment mixture of clay, charcoal, and plaster is first painted carefully over the wax original to make certain that it enters all lines and indentations, entirely covering the form. The whole piece is then placed in a can or other container; the investment material is poured in around it and allowed to harden.

The investment is then placed in a kiln at low temperature (sprue down) to allow all the wax to burn out, hence the term "lost wax."

The investment (which retains the exact negative shape of the wax original) is then ready for the introduction of molten metal. The crucible of melted metal is placed against the mouth of the sprue and the metal is poured into the investment. Today centrifugal casting machines allow for the entry of the metal automatically and rotate the investment in order to force the metal into every section of the mold.

As the metal loses its cherry color, the entire investment is placed into water where the change in temperature causes the investment to crack away, revealing the cast form.

To finish the piece, sprue and vent points must be filed away, and the form must be properly cleaned and polished.

Casting is an art in itself, and most craftsmen send their wax originals to professional casting services. The charges are nominal considering the large investment in equipment that would be necessary if one did one's own casting. Several such services are listed in the Sources of Supply section.

Wax wire offers an enormous range of possibilities. It is, in many respects, much easier to work with than metal wire, and it also offers many extra effects not possible when working directly in wire.

Where hand-soldering could prove tedious and time consuming, wax wire provides a clean easy substitute process. Where hammering and draw-plates are required to flatten and reshape metal wire, hands and small tools suffice for handily manipulating the wax.

Chapter 6

WIRE
AS ARMATURE

Wire outlines. Unembellished and uncluttered forms constructed of wire alone define space just as lines do. Significant forms need not rely upon the complications of design and execution often associated with successful objects. Alexander Calder recognized this in his many whimsical portraits and figures. But these bare skeletons have had a long history as supporting structures for other objects—other forms and materials. Although, when combined with different materials in the ways shown here, the wire is often hidden beneath layers of other substances, the armature remains important. It defines the final shape. The manner of attachment, where it affects the strength of the final form, will be important, too.

At its simplest, the armature becomes the final form as well. The Hostess (1928, 11 1/2″ high), by Alexander Calder. Courtesy: The Museum of Modern Art, gift of Edward M. Warburg.

For the Masai tribeswomen of East Africa, wire serves as the two-dimensional armature for bead necklaces. Wire preserves the circularity and rigidity of the form.

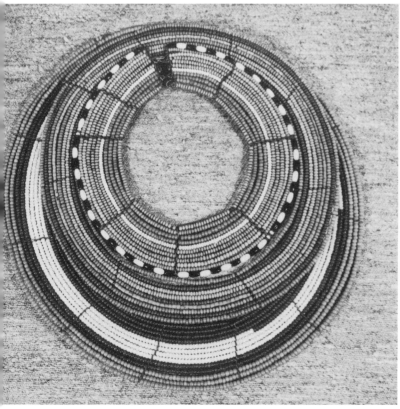

Traditionally, wire served as an armature for papier-mâché and plaster. Modern materials have extended that application. The plastics—acrylic modeling pastes, dipping films, and metal-filled pastes—have provided a new range of possibilities. Each surface treatment has a unique effect on the altered wirework.

PLASTIC FILM

Plastic dipping films, readily available in craft and hobby stores, transform wire armatures from purely linear forms to planar forms. The beauty of these materials is that complex curvilinear surfaces are easily obtainable by sweeping the wire through the fast-drying liquid plastic.

These films require closed wire forms. The wire may be attached in any manner—twisting, soldering, or simply crimping the wire will do, as long as the plane that you wish to define is closed.

After completing several of the items to be coated, open the can and dip. If the forms are too large for the can, pour the plastic into a shallow dish or pan. Since the wire must be drawn through the plastic quickly, smoothly, and continuously, it is wise to plan the operations in advance—especially since most films are solvent-based and dry out quickly when exposed to air. If drying does occur, thin the film with the solvent usually accompanying the product.

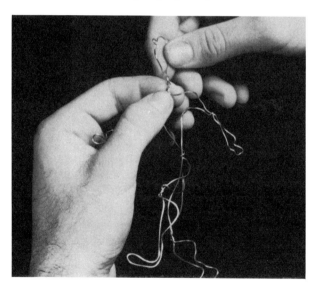

Armatures may be covered with plastic films, which are available in many colors. The outline may be bent and twisted to shape. All areas to be covered must be closed, or the film simply will not cover.

The wire must be immersed completely in the plastic, and the form must be covered completely in a single dipping. Otherwise the plastic will recede. If that does occur, redip the wire immediately. Small forms should cover with little difficulty, but the larger surfaces may require a more considered approach. If, after several attempts, the form simply will not cover, try adding additional cross-supports of wire. These will effectively break the larger surface into smaller units, and since smaller units are easier to cover, better success can be expected.

After dipping, the coated wire must be allowed to dry fully before handling, since even a pinhole in the film during drying will lessen surface tension and collapse the film. One technique, which makes continuous dipping easy, is to stand the newly dipped forms in a block of Styrofoam^R. This will free your hands for the next dipping.

The only structural limitation on this material, as mentioned above, is the fact that the surfaces to be covered cannot be made too large. The design limitations are nonexistent. Because the wire provides structural support, very large combinations of these somewhat smaller elements are possible.

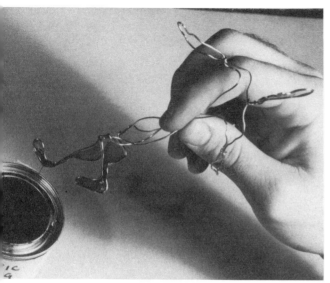

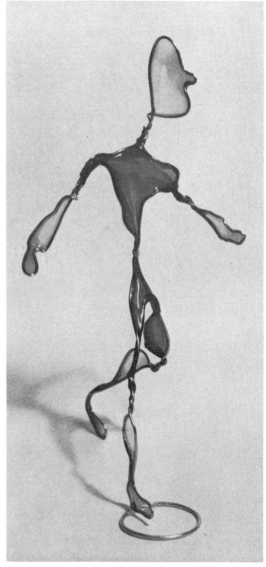

Each section should be dipped into the film in a continuous, sweeping motion. If the plastic pulls away, redip the section immediately. Small areas may be dipped directly into the container, while larger ones may require that the film be transferred to a shallow dish. Do not allow the plastic to be exposed too long, since it thickens as the solvent evaporates. When it becomes too syrupy, thin it with the recommended solvent.

The film covers wire loops, effectively creating planes of translucent colored plastic. While drying, the form may be suspended in a piece of plastic foam, freeing hands for the next pieces.

Imaginative flowers are certainly film stars.

WIRE WRAPPING

A classic application of the wire armature is in wrapped-wire sculpture. The skeleton may be made of almost any type of wire. Heavy wires are recommended for the armature only because they are easily reshaped when the wrapping is complete. The aluminum wire used here is often employed for armatures in sculptures. It is easy to form and re-form later on as the piece progresses.

Wrapping may begin from any convenient point. In the early stages it is wise to wrap on any additional dimensional elements that you intend to make a part of your form. Rather than use excessive amounts of wire in the wrapping process, make a somewhat more fleshed-out form to begin with. In any case, plan to use a lot of wire—wrapping requires large amounts.

There are several methods of wrapping. One is to cut a series of individual pieces, another is to use one continuous piece of wire pulled from a single spool. Either will work well. Combinations of different kinds of wires can also be effective, as can the combination of different gauges in a single form. Exciting effects are also possible when scraps of many different kinds and gauges of wire are combined.

As this form illustrates, wire serves the form without requiring extreme detail. And because wire is so very flexible, the finished sculpture can be shaped and reshaped into many different poses.

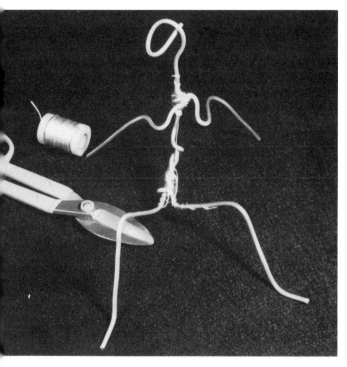

Begin the wrapped-wire sculpture with an armature of heavier wire than the intended wrapping. Aluminum armature wire or coat-hanger wire suits many forms well because they are resilient and light and may be shaped after the wrapping has been completed as well. Joints in the armature are reinforced with thin binding wire.

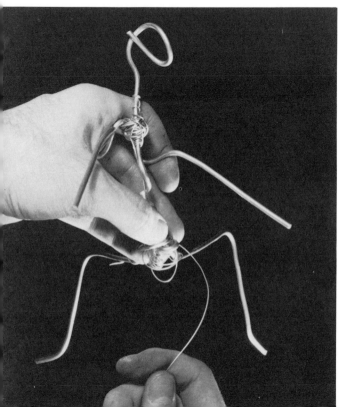

Begin wrapping at any convenient point. Fourteen- and 16-gauge brass and copper wires were used on this form. The early coils should be quite dense, although later layers may be wrapped somewhat more loosely. This makes the entire piece easier to wrap and provides a solid core for the form.

Continue wrapping until the desired dimensionality has been achieved. Do not be deceived by small size—these sculptures require a great deal of wire to complete.

Because the armature and wire are flexible the form may be continually shaped and reshaped after completion.

Mary Lee Hu's Headpiece #4 (1973) is made of wrapped fine silver wire wrapped around a sterling silver wire armature. Courtesy: Mary Lee Hu.

ARMATURE AS FORM

The armature itself can be considered a final form. But as a form it can also undergo slight modifications that alter but preserve the look of wire.

Having found a suitable shape, consider what sort of dimensionality would suit the form. Where should it be thicker and thinner? This curved form, for example, needed additional emphasis and weight. There are several ways of achieving this.

Plaster of Paris will work well, and so will plastic modeling paste. Our choice, however, was a paste called Sculp-metal[R].

Sculp-metal is a thick liquid or paste. Applied with tongue depressors, spatula, or palette knife, it looks like metal when hard.

For the thicknesses we achieved here, several coatings were necessary over a period of several days. Each coat must be allowed to dry sufficiently before applying the next one. (Twenty-four hours is the recommended time between coats.) The length of time, however, will vary with atmospheric conditions. If very thick sections are desired, consider fleshing out the armature form first with additional wire supports. This saves time and, no doubt, the extra wire will be less expensive than the additional Sculp-metal.

The wire armature may be fleshed out by the addition of a paste such as Sculp-metal^R. Begin by bending the wire to shape.

Allow the finished form to dry for a few days or until the coating is absolutely dry and hard to the touch. It is possible at this time to reduce any lumpiness with sandpapers or grinding and sanding bits attached to hand and electric drills. The piece will have a matte finish. But another finishing solution that Sculp-metal is uniquely able to offer is a high shine. To achieve this, burnish (rub) the entire piece (or only accent it, if you prefer) with the back of a spoon and steel wool.

Sculp-metal^R should be applied in thin layers. Use a palette knife or tongue depressor to spread the paste around the wire. Allow each coating to dry thoroughly before applying the next one.

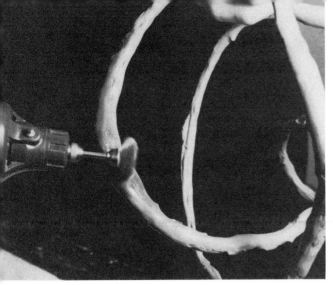

When the desired thickness of covering has been reached, burnish the entire form with a wire brush or steel wool. This produces an overall metallike sheen. The material actually is a mixture involving pulverized metal.

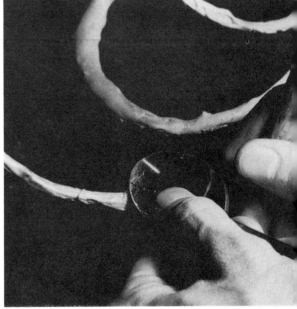

Further accents may be achieved by burnishing selected areas with the back of a spoon; this brings the surface to a high shine.

The final form, which retains the shape of the original wire armature, benefits from the modulation of mass and texture.

PARTIALLY COVERED ARMATURE

This simple Mexican technique of papier-mâché on a complex wire framework is an effective adaptation of the armature concept. It at once preserves the identity of the original wire structure, while adding volume and mass through the partial coverings of paper.

A variety of other materials may be used to partially cover the form: Sculp-metal, plaster of Paris, solder drippings, acrylic modeling paste. The papier-mâché represents an easy, inexpensive, durable, and extremely effective treatment.

The original outline of heavier armature or coat-hanger wire becomes a basis for the network of finer elements. Twist short lengths of wire around the grosser outline to define subtler variations in form.

Cover sections of the completed armature with papier-mâché. Dip torn pieces of paper toweling in a thick mixture of vinyl wallpaper paste, and wrap the strips of paste-laden paper firmly around joints in the wire form. Begin wrapping at the center (interior) of the piece and work outward.

A *stiff wire armature outlines the shape of a kangaroo.*

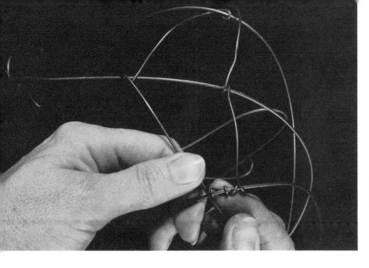

Thinner wire amplifies and strengthens the form.

As much or as little of the structure may be covered as you prefer, but the wiry look of the armature contrasts nicely with the covered sections. Generally, apply only enough papier-mâché to suggest planes and mass.

After the papier-mâché has dried thoroughly, paint the entire piece—wire and all. Acrylic gesso, mixed with acrylic paints, serves the dual purpose of painting the form and of filling gaps and rough spots. If necessary, several coats may be applied, and the acrylics are water soluble when wet, so they readily wash out of brushes and containers.

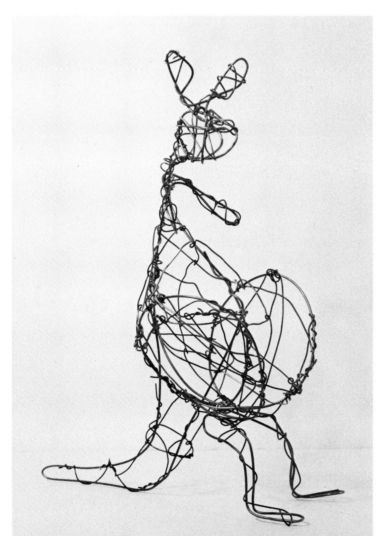

The finished skeleton suggests planes and volumes that will be defined by wrapping with paper.

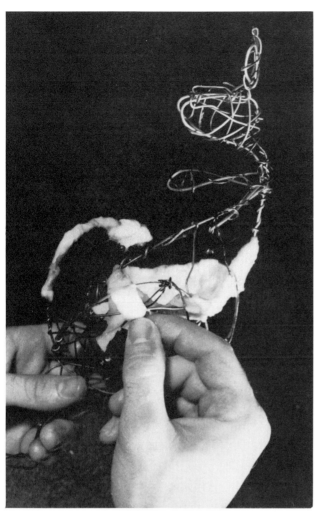

Soak strips of paper toweling in a full-strength mixture of vinyl wallpaper paste (Metylan). Wrapped judiciously around the wire armature, the paper adds mass and planar continuity. Allow the paper to dry thoroughly.

Paint the form with a mixture of acrylic paint and acrylic gesso. The gesso thickens the color, filling gaps and smoothing rough areas in the process.

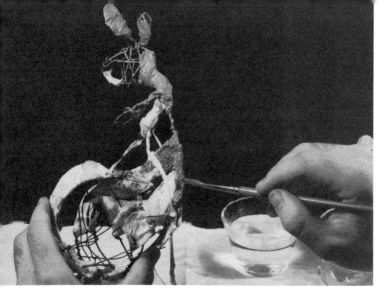

This kangaroo was painted in two
shades of violet.

Finally, the 'roo of the day.

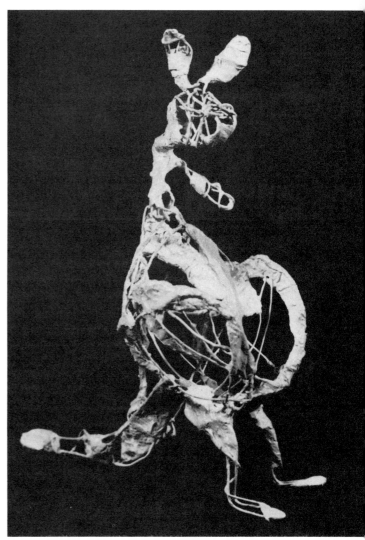

Mexican bird, votive, and bull were constructed in precisely the same way. Both animal forms show good use of internal planes in developing the bodies.

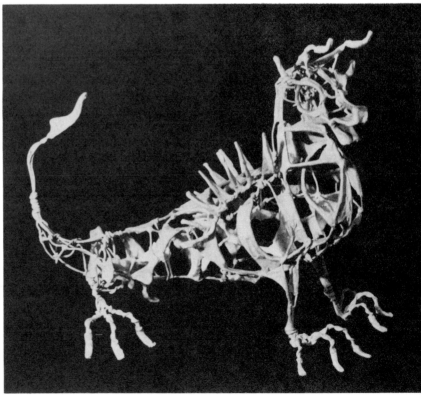

Six-Headed Horse (1953?, 14″ x 14 7/8″), by Germaine Richier, plaster over
string and wire. Collection: The Museum of Modern Art, gift of Katherine Kuh.

Eva Cossock treats armatures with steel wire and solder. Courtesy: Eva Cossock.

WIRE AND PAPER IN RELIEF

In some applications, wire will be completely covered by other materials, but it will remain, as in this *bas-relief,* essential as definer of the final form.

Soldered armatures are most effective in some circumstances. Where three-dimensional contours are emphasized, invisible joints enhance the design.

Process should always be at the back of the designer's mind. In this instance, each section was to be covered with an individual piece of paper. Each section was considered individually to determine whether the span was too great for the curvature and whether the shape and direction of movement fit the overall scheme.

The covering paper, too, was considered carefully. Several possibilities were discarded because they were too heavy when saturated with glue-water, and others were ruled out because they fell apart. All paper is weakened by water, but the paper should not rend too easily, and it must be pliable when wet.

Cut the paper to a shape an inch larger than the space to be covered. Then, dip the entire piece into a solution of white all-purpose glue and water. Smear some full-strength glue on the wire section as well. Place the paper over the armature, stretch it taut, and fold back the margins. With a little squeeze, the paper margins can be made to stick to the back of the paper, holding the piece in place. The paper will tighten on the wire frame as it dries. Repeat this process until the entire framework is covered.

When the paper dries completely, paint the surface with acrylic gesso and paint.

One interesting variation on this process is to use the same wire framework but, instead of using glued paper, sew cloth onto the form.

Binding wire is used to hold wires in place for soldering this armature for a relief sculpture.

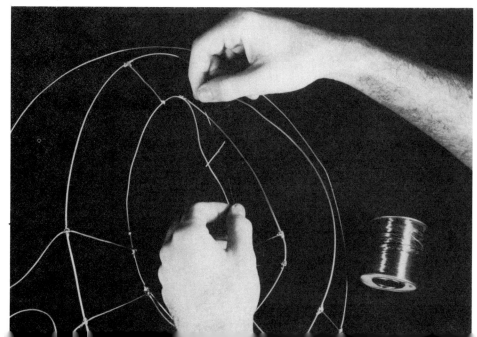

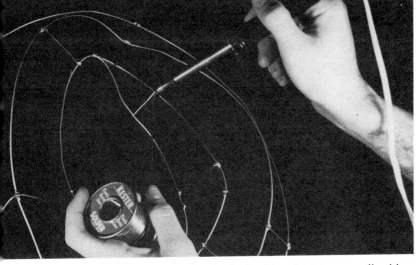

Because of the plethora of individual soldered joints, a small soldering iron and rosin-core soft solder were used to finish the work
quickly. Although soft solder is not very strong, the requirements of
the piece allowed its use. The paper covering will add a great deal
of structural support.

The finished armature has many contours to support the planes that will
extend outward from the plane.

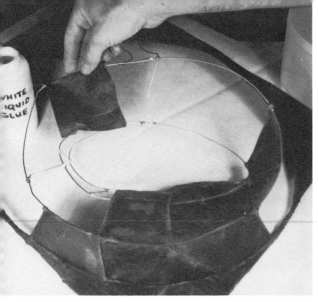

Dip the paper momentarily into a mixture of white glue and water and drape the soft, wet paper over the wires of the armature. Each piece should be cut to cover a particular section with a slight overlap. To assure adhesion, smear some white glue on the wires and then fold back the edges of the paper firmly.

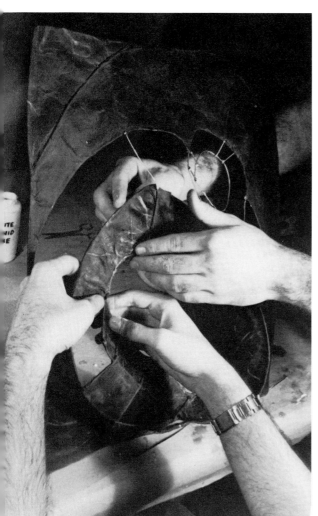

Squeeze the paper back firmly and it will stick to itself and dry in that position, but be careful not to push any fingers through the wet paper.

Allow the paper to dry completely. If the paper was pulled taut over each section during pasting, it should dry to a taut, even surface. This form was painted with acrylic gesso. Acrylic paints may be added to the gesso if color is desired. In the finished relief, the wires are hidden, but their form is traced to a line.

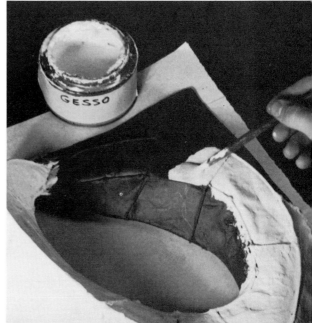

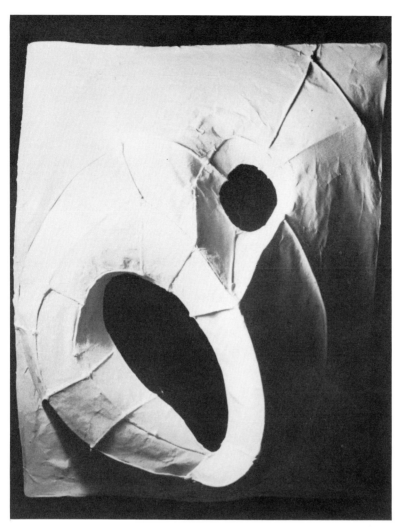

Bas-relief of wire and paper.

Just as paper may be applied over wires, cloth may be sewn over a wire armature. These wire and silk flowers were made in Thailand.

Chapter 7

A GALLERY OF WIRE ART

Engineers and technicians have appreciated wire's utility for decades. As a structural and conductive element, wire remains indispensable. But craftsmen and artists are by far more familiar with the plasticity wire offers.

Wire is an ancient material. Dated nearly to the discovery of metal itself, wire has been a source of inspiration and a vehicle for expression available to artists in every age.

The ideas and processes illustrated in this book recall only the most basic techniques and some few of an infinity of design solutions and creative possibilities.

This chapter groups wire art forms of this age. All were created during the twentieth century. Within this short time span, however, an extraordinary range of wire's qualities has been explored. Wire used alone may define no space at all, concentrating our attentions on planar elements. Alone again, wire may suggest space or volumes or create illusions of time and space. In combination with other materials—glass, paper, metal—wire becomes a structural element, and artists make use of its ready malleability and strength in creating fine planes and larger forms.

Ultimately, wire art needs no explanation. A precious quality of the medium is that the most complex and detailed works remain relatively easy to achieve technically, allowing artist and audience to concentrate on the form and the potential.

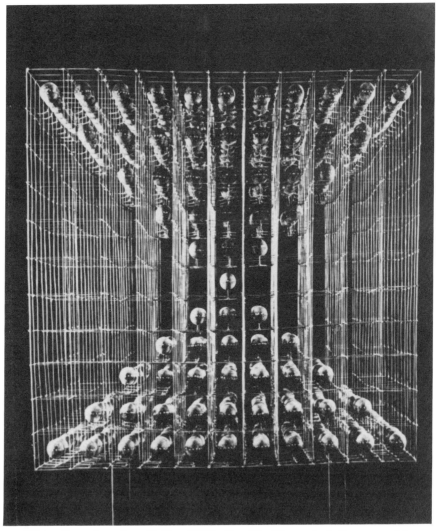

Günter Haese's austere Mekka (1968, 3' x 3') utilizes wire's linear precision.

Harry Kramer defines volumes and internal constructions using soldered wires in Torso. Courtesy: Tate Gallery, London.

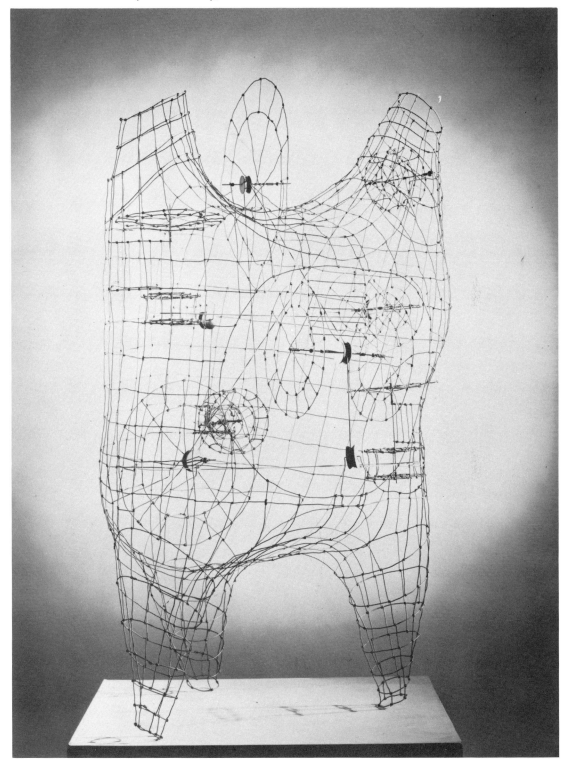

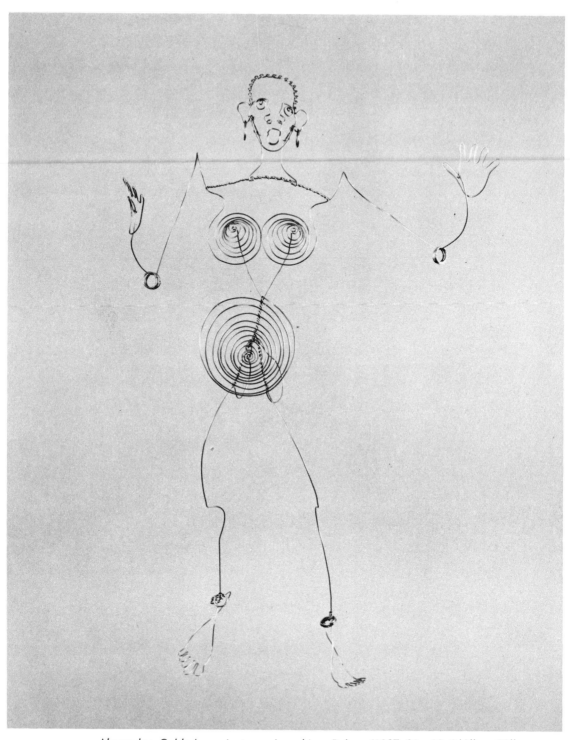

Alexander Calder's caricature, Josephine Baker (1927–29, 22 3/8″ x 39″ x 9 3/4″), capitalizes on the flexibility of fine iron wire. Collection: The Museum of Modern Art.

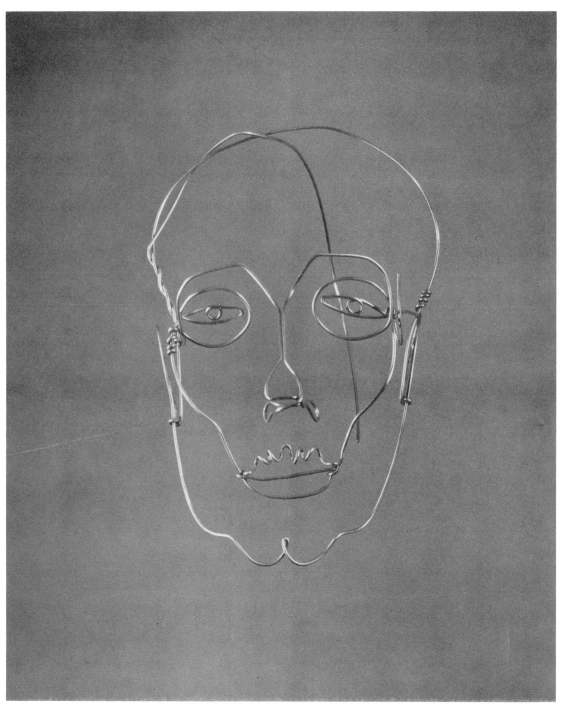

Man with Eyeglasses (1929–30, 12 7/8″ x 8 3/4″ x 13 1/2″), also by Calder, is not meant for frontal viewing alone. The visage changes when viewed from different angles. Collection: The Museum of Modern Art.

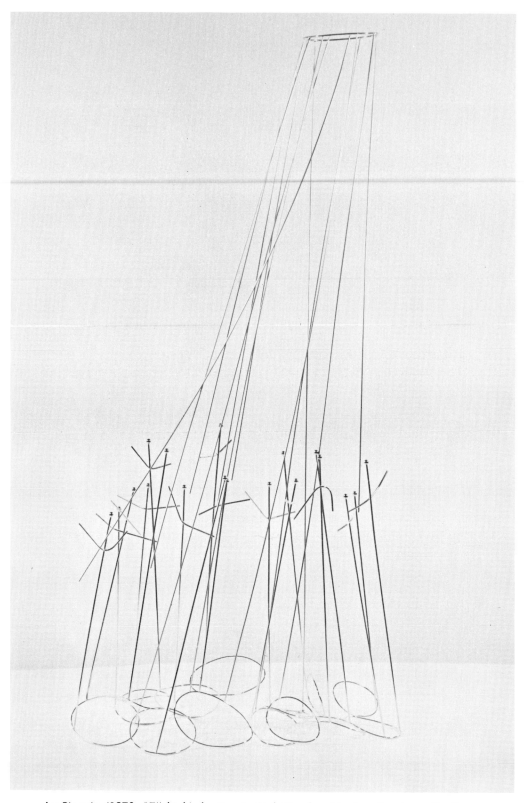

La Pioggia (1970, 17″ high), by Fausto Melotti, of gold wire. Courtesy: Marlborough Gallery.

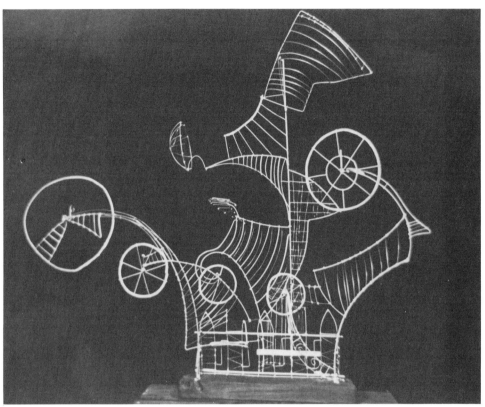

La Nonne, a construction of bronze, brass, and copper wires by Juan Luis Bunuel.
Courtesy: Willard Gallery.

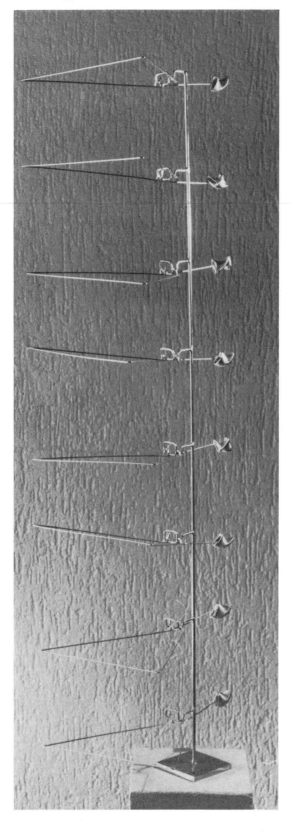

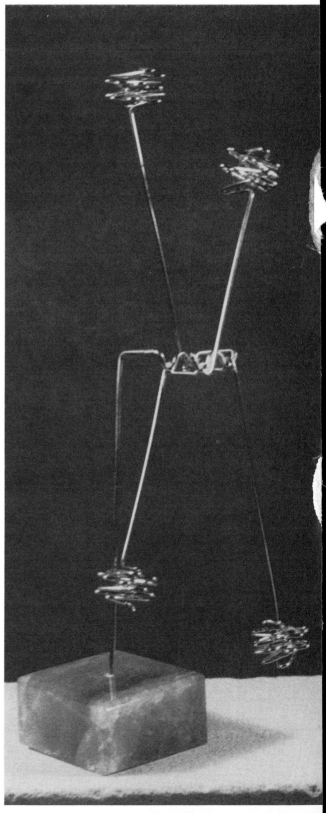

Column of Triangles with Spirals (1973, 18" x 6"), by George Rickey. Gilded triangles of stainless steel wire float and bob around their wire axis. Courtesy: George Rickey.

George Rickey's Four Spirals (1971) of silver wire swing like pendulums. Courtesy: George Rickey.

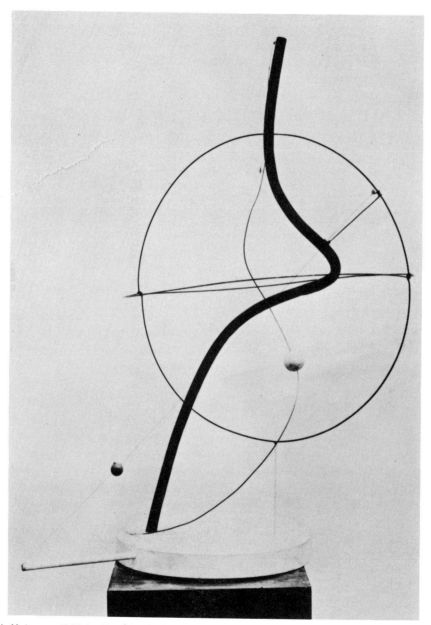

A Universe (1934, 40 1/2" high) is Alexander Calder's motorized mobile of iron pipe, wire, string, and wood. Collection: The Museum of Modern Art, gift of Abby Aldrich Rockefeller.

In an introduction to a Calder exhibition, Jean Paul Sartre wrote: "Sculpture suggests movement, painting suggests depth or light. A 'mobile' does not 'suggest' anything: it captures genuine living movements and shapes them." This shaper of space is Lobster Trap and Fish Tail (1939, 8'6" x 9'6"). Collection: The Museum of Modern Art.

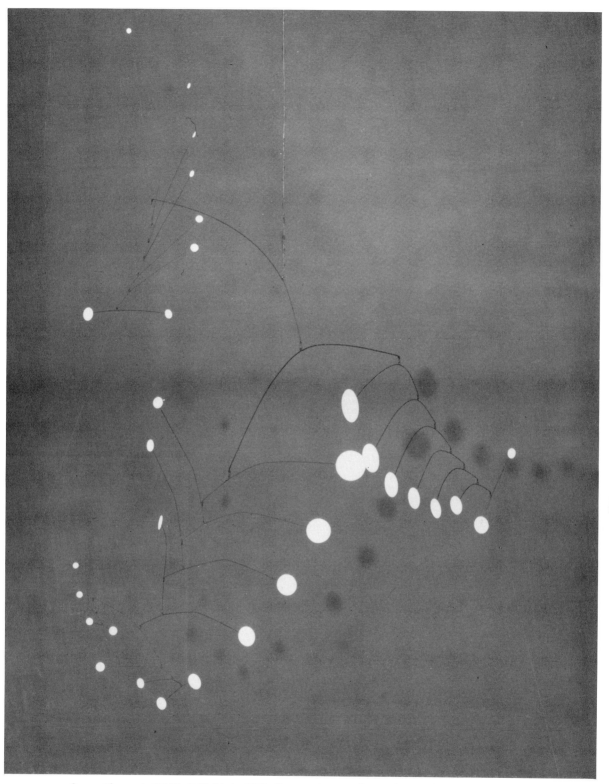

Snow Flurry I (1948, 94" high, 70" diameter) reminds us that Calder once re-
marked that "the idea of an object floating—not supported—the use of a very long
thread, or a long arm in cantilever as a means of support seems best to approximate this freedom from the earth." Collection: The Museum of Modern Art.

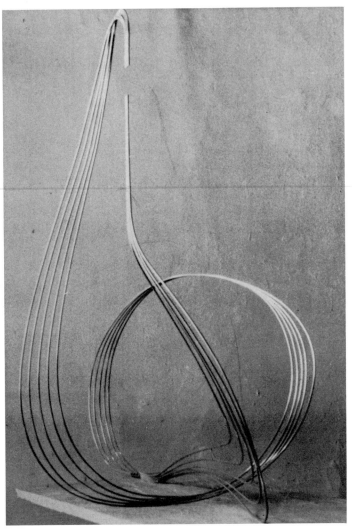

The smoothly flowing brass wires in Richard Lippold's
Embrace (1947, 40″ high) suggest one aspect of the
artist's fascination with this medium. Courtesy: Willard
Gallery.

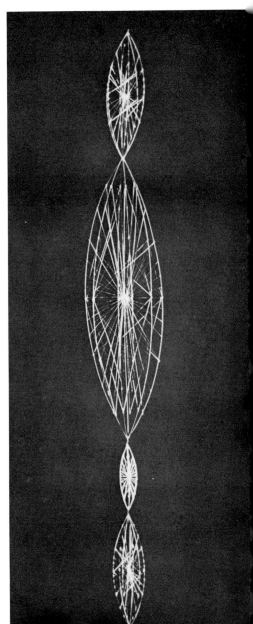

Lippold's Dew Pendant (1972, 24″ x 4″) of gold and
silver wires suggests another inspiration entirely. Courtesy: Willard Gallery.

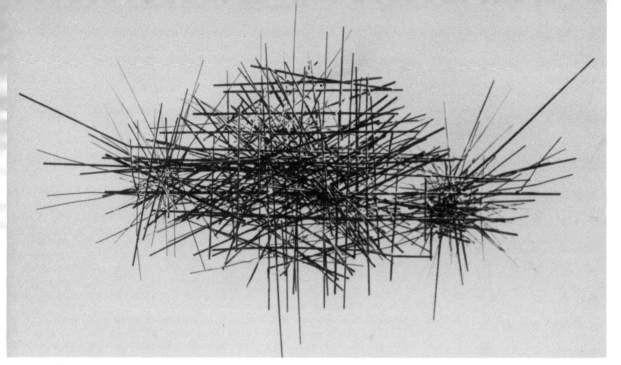

Phoenix Desert (1973, 15' long), by
Herbert Feuerlicht, constructed of
braised steel rod and wire. Copyright
Herbert A. Feuerlicht.

A study in steel wire. Copyright Herbert A. Feuerlicht.

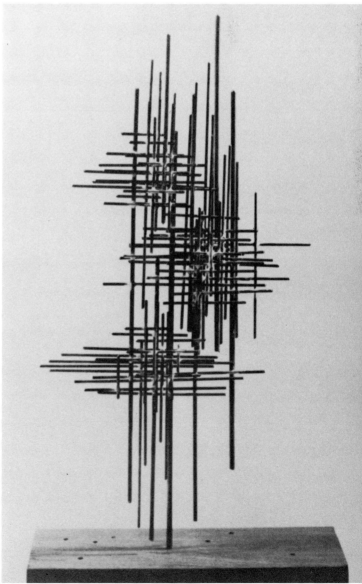

Sunset I (1953, 19 1/4" high), stone and painted wire by David Hare. Collection: The Museum of Modern Art.

The Seed (1959, 7 1/2" x 5" x 5"), gold and stainless steel wires, by Richard Lippold. Courtesy: Willard Gallery.

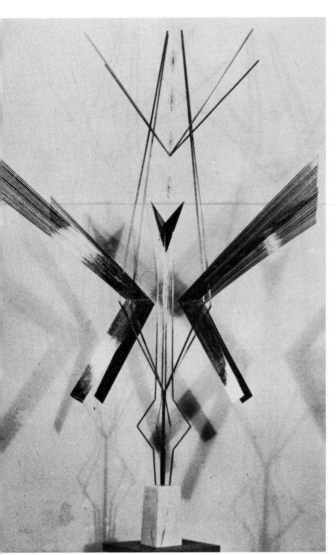

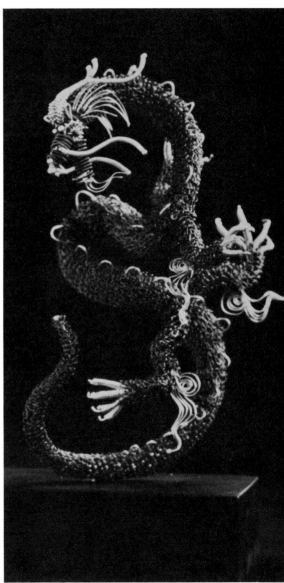

As in many of Richard Lippold's pieces, the parallel wires that appear as planes in Man (1973) will shift and disappear into a single line as the viewer passes around the sculpture. Courtesy: Willard Gallery.

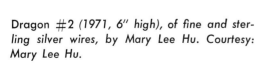

Dragon #2 (1971, 6" high), of fine and sterling silver wires, by Mary Lee Hu. Courtesy: Mary Lee Hu.

Mary Lee Hu's Aquatic Insect Larva (1971, 9" long), of fine silver and precoated copper wires. Courtesy: Mary Lee Hu.

The Turtle (1968, 5" x 7"), of wrapped and woven fine silver wire. Courtesy: Mary Lee Hu.

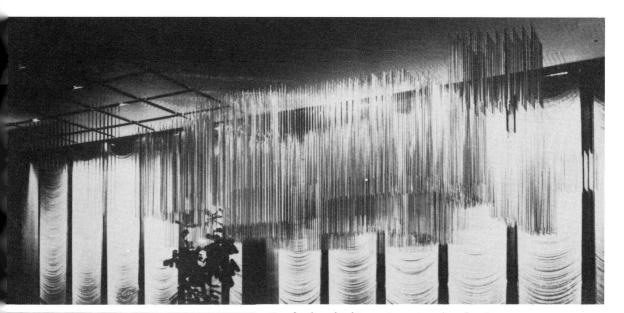

Hundreds of shimmering strands of wire compose Richard Lippold's sculpture for the Seagram Building in New York. Courtesy: Willard Gallery.

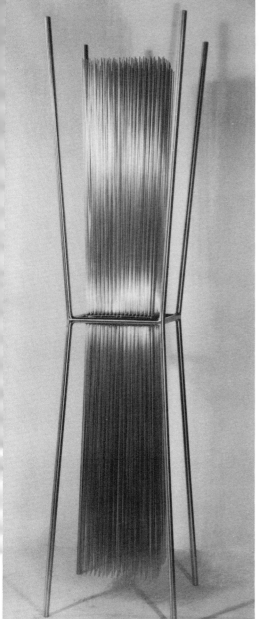

Elemental units of wire extend like stalactites and stalagmites from the center of Harry Bertoia's Untitled (1960, 83" x 20" x 20"). Courtesy: Staempfli Gallery.

227

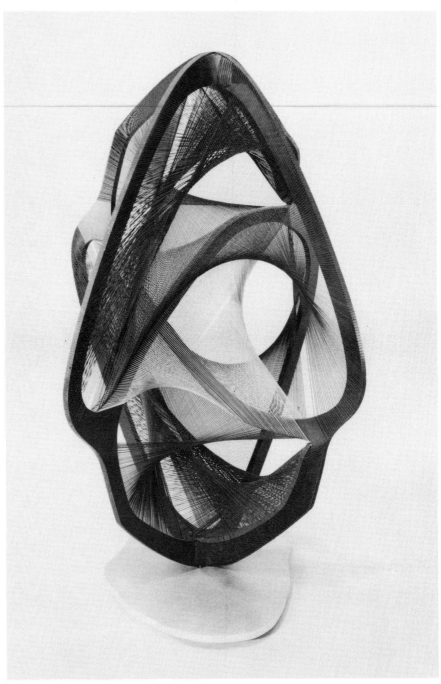

*Naum Gabo's Linear Construction No. 4 in Black and Gray (1950, 33" x 27")
capitalizes on wire's pliancy in creating complex curves around a rigid framework.
The work is of steel and aluminum. Courtesy: The Art Institute of Chicago.*

According to Norbert Kricke: "Open space and lines [are] a form of movement, representing our reality: space-time. Space and time forms are one unity and impossible to separate." Since 1950 Mr. Kricke has developed forms for use with water. Space Sculpture (1964), of welded stainless steel rods, stands thirty feet high. Courtesy: Los Angeles County Museum of Art.

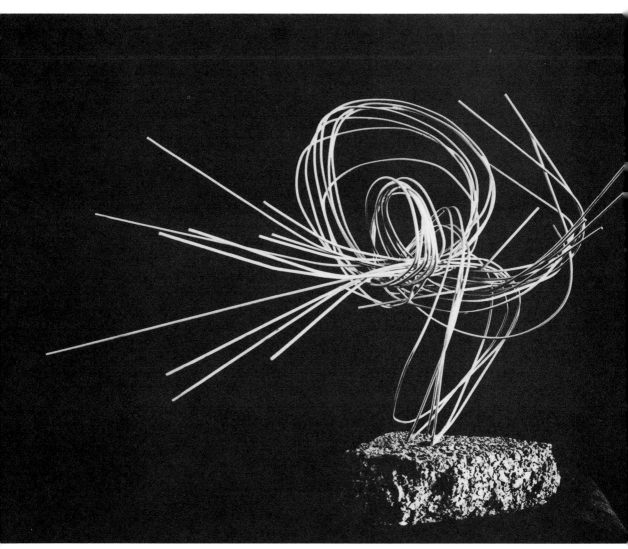

Norbert Kricke writes: "In my sculpture I use wire as line, but lines are never used in a way to make contours of a mass-form." This piece, constructed in 1955–56, is in nickel wire (12" high x 20" long). Courtesy: Norbert Kricke.

In contrast to Kricke, the works of the Matschinsky-Denninghoffs do not preserve line, but, rather, incorporate lines into mass. This is one of their smaller pieces; made of brass and tin wires, it stands one foot tall. Courtesy: Matschinsky-Denninghoff.

Labyrinth (1965, 2′ x 1′ x 1′), welded brass wire, by Matschinsky-Denninghoff.
Courtesy of the artists, photograph by Martin Matschinsky.

Harlekin (1972, 12′ tall), by Matschinsky-Denninghoff, is constructed of welded stainless-steel tubes. Courtesy of the artists.

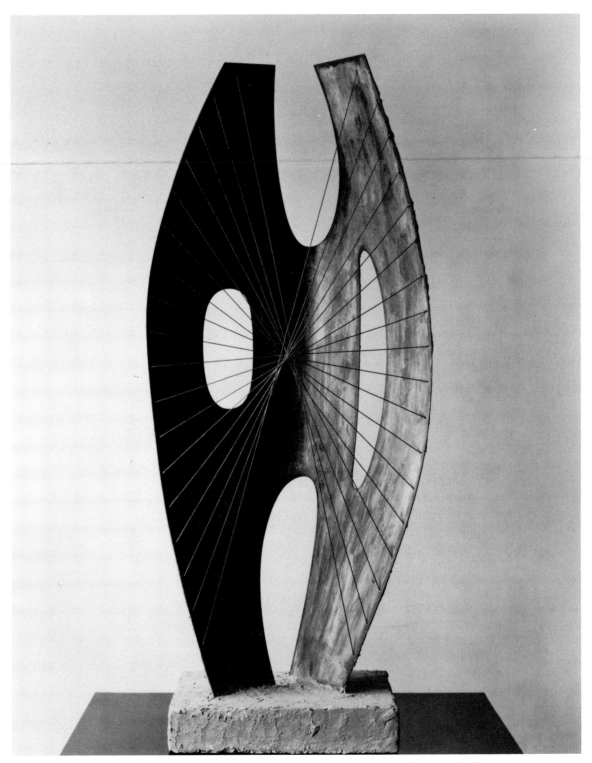

Winged Figure, by Barbara Hepworth. Courtesy: Vassar College Art Gallery.

GLOSSARY

Acrylic gesso/acrylic modeling paste

Acrylic media which may be used to patch, fill, and model wire forms. Modeling paste is especially effective in building up wires. The gesso makes a good protective coating and finish. Both may be colored with acrylic paints.

Alloy

A combination of two or more metals.

Annealing

Heating a metal to a temperature below its melting point in order to relieve stresses caused by wiredrawing or cold forging.

Anvil

A block of metal, usually iron, with a hardened steel top, against which metals are forged while cold or hot.

Armature

A skeleton used as supporting structure for other materials.

Burnishing

A polishing or shaping operation carried on with the aid of an extremely hard tool known as the burnisher, usually made of steel, hematite, agate, or bloodstone.

Casting

Introducing a liquid, which will soon solidify, into a space within another material.

Chasing

A metal-decorating technique using punches forced into the surface of metal with a hammer.

Clear flux

Uncolored powdered glass used in enameling as the initial and binding layer over the raw material.

Cloisonné

From the French word *cloison,* or "partition," the process of attaching flat wires to metal in such a way as to partition areas that are then filled with enamels of different colors. The individual sections are known as *cloisons.*

Cold solder

A metal-colored adhesive for attaching metal parts.

Corrosion

Gradual degradation of metals caused by moisture, air, chemicals.

Counterenameling

The process of enameling the underside of metal to be enameled in order to eliminate cracking due to differing contraction-expansion ratios on either side of the form.

Crucible

A container, most often made of a refractory material like clay, used to hold metal about to be melted and during melting.

Cure

Or *set* is the process by which the physical properties of a plastic change. In polyester and epoxy resins the cure is effected by a catalyst that triggers chemical reactions which allow the plastics to solidify.

Drawplate

A steel plate with tapered holes of successively decreasing/increasing diameter used to reduce the diameter of wire.

Drawtongs

Tongs with heavy clamp jaws and a hooked handle, used to grip and pull wire through the drawplate.

Ductility

The measure of a metal's characteristics determined by the fineness to which it may be drawn into wire.

Embedment

Casting or laminating an object within a block or layer of usually clear resin.

Enamel

Powdered glass that is fused onto the surface of metals in cloisonné, or into fine, transparent units suspended by flat wires in plique-à-jour. Enamels are available in hundreds of colors and in transparent, translucent, and opaque varieties.

Enameling oil (lavender oil)

Applied to the surface of metal to be enameled to hold clear flux to the form. It is often used to hold the enamel in place during firing on vertical or curved surfaces. During firing it flames up and burns off almost immediately.

Epoxy adhesive

An especially versatile and strong adhesive, usually available in two parts—resin and hardener—to be mixed in equal quantities. Two-part epoxies are now available in quick-hardening form: they set in three to five minutes. The normal epoxy sets overnight. Both require twenty-four hours to fully cure and reach full strength.

Epoxy resins

Are of the same general group as epoxy adhesives, except that particular resins may be chosen for their specific qualities (enumerated by the manufacturer). The epoxy must still be mixed with a hardener, or catalyst, although usually not in equal parts. Epoxy resin is especially valuable in applications requiring minimal shrinkage, as with plastic plique-à-jour.

Extrusion

A method for creating continuous strands or units by forcing molten or viscous material through a die.

Filigree

An ornamental technique utilizing fine wires soldered in open designs.

Fire scale

An oxide that forms on or immediately below the surface of metal, usually because of overheating. This may be avoided, in soldering or annealing, by applying flux to the form. In enameling, apply an anti-scalant to the nonenameled surface. To remove scaling if it occurs, buff or use pickling solution.

Flux

A liquid, paste, or powder that helps dissolve and hinders the subsequent production of oxides on metals. In soldering it is a mandatory vehicle for solder, not only cleaning and keeping the metal clean, but to some extent holding solder in place on the form. The most commonly used fluxes are made of borax.

Forging

The process of shaping and/or forming metals by hammering against a hard metal block or an anvil. Forging may be carried out while the metal is hot or cold. Cold-forged metals must be annealed to restore original pliancy, because hammering makes them hard and brittle.

Gauge

A measure of the diameter of materials, especially wires and sheet metals. Brown & Sharpe is the standard measuring system now in use for wires.

Gel

An intermediate stage in the curing process of resin evidenced by a gelatinlike appearance. In the gel state, the resin has taken shape, but has not yet fully cured.

Hard solder

Also known as silver solder, as opposed to *soft* solder which is made of lead and melts at considerably lower temperatures. Hard solder is available in four grades, each melting at a different temperature. It is also available in different colors for silver and gold alloys.

Jig

A form used as a guide or model in shaping wires. The simplest jigs consist of nails driven into wood. More precise jigs may be constructed of wood or metal, and commercial jigs for bending wire to particular shapes are also available.

Karat

A measure of the gold content of gold alloys. Twenty-four-karat gold equals 100 percent gold; twelve-karat indicates 50 percent gold and 50 percent alloy, and so on. Not to be confused with the word *carat* used in referring to gems.

Kiln

An enclosed furnace usually lined with a refractory material like clay, capable of reaching high temperatures. Kilns are often used for annealing wires, and they are invariably used in enameling. Enameling kilns are special units, designed to allow the artisan to constantly monitor the course of firing. All kilns reach high temperatures and should be used in controlled and ventilated surroundings.

Linear

A term used to describe elements and forms that suggest lines of line drawings.

Liver of sulphur

A chemical used to oxidize and color metals quickly. When using any colorant, experiment on a nonvisible surface or a piece of scrap to determine whether the proper effect will be achieved with that material. Different metals react differently to the same chemical.

Lost-wax casting process

A modeled wax form is melted from a mold, leaving a cavity that is then filled with another material, usually metal.

Malleability

That measure of a metal's characteristics describing the ability to be formed by hammering or rolling.

Mandrel

A metal rod available in many shapes, most often tapered. It forms an effective base for forming chains, rings, bracelets, and other pieces that require specific and precise circumference.

Melting point

The temperature at which a substance liquefies.

Oxide

The substance that forms when oxygen combines chemically with metal. The process of oxidation is hastened by heating metal.

Pickle

A solution of one part sulphuric acid and ten parts water used after soldering to dissolve flux and oxide buildup. It may also be used as a metal cleaner in preparation for soldering and enameling. Non-acidic metal cleaners like Sparex^R are available too. The acid solution works best when heated slightly. And, as a precaution, *never* add water to acid. Always add acid to water—otherwise the splatters may sputter.

Plique-á-jour

A rarefied enameling procedure in which transparent enamels are placed within very small cloisons of flat wire. The flat wire form rests on a thin sheet of mica which provides a backing and firing surface. The technique is a difficult one to master.

Polyester resins

A primary difference between polyesters and epoxies is that polyesters tend to shrink more and should not be used where shrinkage is critical. *See Epoxy resins.*

Poly-Mosaic^R tiles

Fusible plastic tiles that are easily cut and fused in a home oven. They are readily available in a wide range of brilliant transparent and opaque colors. See Sources of Supply.

Quenching

Rapid cooling of heated metal, most often accomplished by dunking in water or pickle solution.

Solder

A metal or metal alloy used to join metal parts.

Soldering

A technique for joining metals with alloys that flow into joints at a temperature lower than the melting point of the metal being soldered. *See Hard solder.*

Torch

Refers to variety of heat sources that produce a more or less neutral flame, including propane torch, acetylene torch, oxyacetylene torch.

Wax wire

Wires of wax, available in many hardnesses, gauges, shapes, for use in the lost-wax casting process.

Welding

The process of heating metals to their melting points and causing them to fuse together.

Wire

Metal, usually in the form of a very flexible thread or slender rod.

Wiredrawing

The process of reducing the diameter of wire or changing the shape of wire by drawing it through holes of successively decreasing diameter in a steel drawplate.

Wire Screening

A woven mesh of fine wires, most often aluminum, copper, steel, or brass.

BIBLIOGRAPHY

Barber, Clifford L. *Solder: Its Fundamentals and Usage.* Chicago: Kester Solder Company, Third Division, 1965.

Gentille, Thomas. *Step-by-Step Jewelry.* New York: Golden Press, 1968.

Gruber, Elmar. *Metal & Wire Sculpture.* New York: Sterling Publishing Company, Inc., 1973.

Lidstone, John. *Building with Wire.* New York: Van Nostrand Reinhold, 1972.

Lynch, John. *How to Make Mobiles.* New York: Viking Press, 1970.

Meilach, Dona Z., and Seiden, Donald. *Direct Metal Sculpture.* New York: Crown Publishers, Inc., 1966.

Morris, John D. *Creative Metal Sculpture.* New York: Bruce Publishing Company, 1971.

Newman, Jay Hartley and Lee Scott. *Plastics for the Craftsman.* New York: Crown Publishers, Inc., 1972.

Newman, Thelma R. *Plastics as Craft.* Radnor, Pa.: Chilton Books, 1975.

————. *Wax as an Art Form.* New Brunswick, N. J.: Thomas Yoseloff, 1966.

Newman, Thelma R., Jay Hartley, and Lee Scott. *Paper as Art and Craft.* New York: Crown Publishers, Inc., 1973.

Sommer, Elyse. *Contemporary Costume Jewelry.* New York: Crown Publishers, Inc., 1974.

Stribling, Mary Lou. *Art From Found Materials.* New York: Crown Publishers, Inc., 1970.

Untracht, Oppi. *Metal Techniques for Craftsmen.* New York: Doubleday & Company, 1968.

Ziek, Nona. *Making Silver Jewelry.* New York: Lancer Books, 1973.

SOURCES OF SUPPLY

Wires and wireworking tools are readily available everywhere. There are few specialized products, and craft, art, and hobby stores always carry basic wire-stuffs and solders, pliers, and tweezers and saws.

The sources listed in this section are either direct suppliers—usually by mail as well—or manufacturers. Direct suppliers, of course, are more than happy to sell their products, and manufacturers will invariably tell consumers where they may purchase supplies in their own areas.

General Supplies

Abbey Materials Corporation
116 West 29th Street
New York, New York 10001
> Complete line of tools, wires, buffs, hammers, wax wires and sheets, drawplates, and solders. Will mail order. Catalog.

Allcraft Tool and Supply Co., Inc.
15 West 45th Street
New York, New York 10036
> and
215 Park Avenue
Hicksville, New York 11801
> Complete line of wires and materials for nearly every craft, especially enameling (cloisonné, plique-à-jour). Mail order. A favorite of craftsmen.

Anchor Tool & Supply Company
231 Main Street
Chatham, New Jersey 07928

Brookstone Company
Peterborough, New Hampshire 03458
> One of the largest (and best) suppliers by mail. Sells a complete line of wires, solders, fine tools. Catalog.

CCM Arts and Crafts, Inc.
9520 Baltimore Avenue
College Park, Maryland 20740
> Complete line of suppliers for the wireworker.

Craftool Company
1 Industrial Road
Woodbridge, New Jersey 07095
> Tools and equipment.

240

Sax Arts and Crafts
207 N. Milwaukee Street
Milwaukee, Wisconsin 53202

Wireworking Tools

Dremel Tools
Racine, Wisconsin 53406
    A complete line of effective, ingenious, and efficient tools for working
    with many media. Flexible shaft drills especially useful in grinding and
    polishing.

Tools Unlimited, Inc.
P. O. Box 7
Brentwood, New York 11717
    Wire bending jigs, and a large assortment of interesting and useful
    tools.

Vinkemulder Tool Co.
2223 Estelle Dr. S. E.
Grand Rapids, Michigan 49506
    Ratchet handle wire bender

See above: Abbey, Allcraft, Anchor, Brookstone, and Craftool.

Wax Wire

    Many of the supply sources listed above do sell many varieties of waxes
and wax wires, but a primary manufacturer is

Kerr Dental Manufacturing Co.
6081–6095 12th Street
Detroit, Michigan

Findings and Chains
Eastern Findings Corporation
19 West 34th Street
New York, New York 10001

Metal Findings Corporation
152 West 22nd Street
New York, New York 10011

Universal Chain Co.
110 West 34th Street
New York, New York 10001

Solders

Solders are readily available throughout this country and the world. Hardware stores, the suppliers listed above, and most craft and art stores carry many varieties. Some manufacturers are listed here:

Duratite Division of DAP
General Offices
1504 North Gettysburg
Dayton, Ohio 45427
    Duratite liquid solder.

Kester Solder Company
Division of Litton Industries
4201 Wrightwood Avenue W.
Chicago, Illinois 60639

LePages
Pittsburgh, Pennsylvania 15238
    Liquid solder.

Casting Services

Casting services exist in nearly every city. They do vary in quality, but most are at least competent. Those listed here will also work by mail, although, when possible, it is advisable to at least deliver the fragile wax model by hand.

Billanti Casting Company
64 West 48th Street
New York, New York 10036

Plastic Paintable Mediums
M. Grumbacher, Inc.
460 West 34th Street
New York, New York 10001
    "Hyplar" acrylic polymer latex emulsion paste.

Hunt Manufacturing Co.
New Masters Fine Art Division
Statesville, North Carolina 28677
    "Vanguard" polymer paint, gesso, and modeling paste.

Permanent Pigments
Cincinnati, Ohio 45201
    "Liquitex" polymer medium, gesso, and modeling paste.

Plastic Putties
Devcon Corporation
Danvers, Massachusetts 01923

    Plastic steel and epoxy bond, steel- and aluminum-filled pastes.

Sculp-metal Co.
701 Investment Building
Pittsburgh, Pennsylvania 15222
    Metal-filled paste: "Sculp-metal."

Poly-Mosaic Fusible Plastic Tiles

Ain Plastics
65 Fourth Avenue
New York, New York 10003

Boin Arts & Crafts
91 Morris Street
Morristown, New Jersey 07960

CCM Arts & Crafts
9520 Baltimore Avenue
College Park, Maryland 20740

Dick Blick Co.
Box 1267
Galesburg, Illinois 61401

Economy Arts and Crafts
47-11 Francis Lewis Blvd.
Flushing, New York 11361

Industrial Plastics
324 Canal Street
New York, New York 10013

Poly-Dec Co., Inc.
P. O. Box 541
Bayonne, New Jersey 07002

Sax Arts and Crafts
207 N. Milwaukee Street
Milwaukee, Wisconsin 53202

Plastic Dipping Film

Flexcraft Industries
527 Avenue P & Wilson
Newark, New Jersey 07105

Plastic Resins

Polyester and epoxy resins are available from plastics suppliers and hardware stores. They are generally too heavy to be mail-ordered, except for small amounts of epoxy casting resin.

Ain Plastics
65 Fourth Avenue
New York, New York 10003

Cadillac Plastics and Chemical Co.
15841 Second Avenue, P. O. Box 810
Detroit, Michigan

A complete assortment of plastic resins and products—and outlets throughout the country and North America.

INDEX

(Figures in *italics* refer to illustrations.)